Holy Spirit

Holy Spirit

THE PROMISE. THE PRESENCE. THE POWER.

Dr. Mary J. Bryant

Dove 378

Contents

notes   1

One
Dedication   2

Two
This Book Belongs to   4

Three
Acknowledgements   5

Four
Featured Testimonies About the Holy Spirit   7

Five
Foreward   14

Six
Introduction   16

Seven
Prayer   20

Eight
The Promise. The Presence. The Power   21

Nine
Holy Spirit - Get to Know Him   25

Ten
Jesus and the Holy Spirit   33

Eleven
The Three Cs of the Holy Spirit: 39

Twelve
The Holy Spirit and Salvation   51

Thirteen
The Holy Spirit and the Cross   58

Fourteen
Acts of the Holy Spirit   66

Fifteen
The Holy Spirit -the Power of the Church   71

Sixteen
The Spirit and the (s)Word   85

Seventeen
Life through the [Holy] Spirit   91

Eighteen
Walking in the [Holy] Spirit   99

Nineteen
Love Poured Out by the Holy Spirit   112

Twenty
The Symbols of The Holy Spirit   118

Twenty-One
The Outpouring of the Holy Spirit and the Global Release of
God's Glory   120

Twenty-Two
Conclusion   126

Twenty-Three
Afterward   131

Twenty-Four
From Dr. Mary J. Bryant   133

Twenty-Five
About the author   136

Twenty-Six
Other Books   138

The Holy Spirit: The Promise. The Presence. The Power

Copyright © 2022 Dr. Mary J. Bryant

Dr. Mary J. Bryant, Author

Edited by Elaine Miles Dupree

The Author's inside photo taken by Michael A. Bryant, Sr. and Back cover photo by Dion's HD Video & Photo Productions (803-942-1259)

All Scripture from the King James Version unless otherwise noted.

One

∽

Dedication

This book is dedication to my sister, **Reverend Lessie W. Loadholt**. She didn't get a chance to see my finished work. When I told her it was about the Holy Spirit, she said that this is going to be a "good one". We love you! Gone but never forgotten.

Poem of Life

Life is but a stopping place,
A pause in what is to be,
A resting place along the road,
to sweet eternity.
We all have different journeys,
Different paths along the way,
We all were meant to learn some things,
but never meant to stay...
Our destination is a place,
Far greater than we know.
For some the journey is quicker,
For some the journey is slow.
And when the journey finally ends,
We'll claim a great reward,
And find an everlasting peace,
Together with the Lord.

Two

~

This Book Belongs to

_____

Three

∾

Acknowledgements

Gratefulness is flowing from my heart. This has really been a lesson in perseverance and endurance in completing this book. I give all glory and honor to God Father, God Savior, and God Holy Spirit because I could not have done this without Them. Many times, over these three plus years I thought about not finishing this book. Only by the Grace of God I could press my way through. "He who calls is faithful and will do it." (1st Thessalonians 5:24).

I thank God for my family, my husband Michael Bryant, Sr, our children Michael Bryant, Jr. (Savannah); Megan Bryant Belin (Jarvis & Janiah); Marquis Bryant and our granddaughter Michaela Bryant. I am grateful to each one of them.

A big God Bless you and thank you to these ladies who thought it not robbery to share their testimony about the Holy Spirit: Minister Megan Belin, Sister Eugenia Gordon, Prophet Shirley Ford, Reverend Marcella Scott, Elder Terrilyn Shorter and Rev. Dr. Margo Williams.

I owe gratitude to Elaine Dupree Miles for providing editing for the book. Thank Elaine! God bless you and give you the desires of your heart.

I also am grateful for those who are members of my Facebook group: Mary's Author's Corner.

An extra thanks and God Bless you to Prophet Shirley E. Ford who always comes through for me and Michael A. Bryant for all his support.

I also thank all who will purchase this book. **God Bless each of you!**

Four

~

Featured Testimonies About the Holy Spirit

I was inspired to invite others to share their testimony about their relationship with Holy Spirit and feature them in my book. Surprising, I didn't receive as many responses as I thought I would have. But I leave it to God. None of these testimonies are altered. I have left them the way they were sent to me by each person. I pray that you will be blessed by them.

Testimony Contributed by:

- Minister Megan J. Belin
- Sister Eugenia Gordon
- Reverend Marcella Scott
- Prophet Shirley E. Ford
- Elder Terrilyn Shorter
- Rev. Dr. Margo W. Williams
- Rev. Dr. Mary J. Bryant

Testimony by Minster Megan J. Belin

For years I lived my life in complete and total darkness. I was walking in circles daily. I never knew that I was dying every day. I didn't believe

I deserved anything more or better. There were nights I cried myself to sleep. There were nights I wasn't sure if I wanted to live.

For years my mother talked to me about Jesus. Here is a man that gave His life for mine and I could not accept His perfect love for me. I could not accept this abundant life that was mine for the taking. I would listen to my mother, but I never really heard her. I was simply humoring her out of respect.

I remember one night in particular I was lying in bed after putting my two-year-old daughter to sleep and I just started crying. I couldn't call anyone; I couldn't even speak. I felt lost. I felt so alone. I couldn't call my mom. I couldn't call my friends. I was pretty much crying hysterically. After what felt like hours of sobbing into my pillow, I felt the soft touch of a hand. I was afraid at first. I wasn't sure. The hand touched my face so gently. I wiped my face and set up in my bed. I just began to smile. I knew at that moment I wasn't alone. I knew at that moment there was a presence in my room. I wasn't sure, but I was at peace.

The next morning, I went to church. The Pastor used the scripture Psalm 56:8. The scripture says, "You keep track of all my sorrows. You have collected all my tears in your bottle. You have recorded each one in your book." I knew that the night before I was loved by His Holy Spirit. I knew I wasn't alone. I knew I was worthy of His love. I knew I was worthy of His perfect peace.

I love the Holy Spirit. I love how gentle He is with me. I love that He is always present within me. I love that He is gentle. I love that He corrects me. I love my relationship with the Holy Spirit. I will always remember my initial encounter with Him.

I cherish my relationship with the Holy Spirit. **Minster Megan J. Belin**

Testimony by Eugenia Gordon

Well my first meeting with the holy spirit, was one night, many years ago, I was really feeling down, and crying, watching Juanita Bynum, on T.V. and all of a sudden, something more powerful, then I have ever known or felt, came upon me, and within me, I was drunk, but I wasn't drinking, it was a beautiful high, from the holy spirit, letting me know within me with my spirit, that I am a child of God, now I was so excited, feeling the joy of the Lord inside of me, my spirit and the Holy Spirit-spirit together, I must tell you, that is a feeling that's so light and so glorious, my God, the very next morning, I had to tell someone, about this heavenly joy that had happen to me, so I quickly ran as fast as I could to my mom's house, to tell her, but I was laughing and carrying on, mom didn't knew what to think, because my joy was so out of this world, and ever since that night, something truly changed in my person, now I know that the holy spirit lives within me he is my help, my paraclete, ...The Shekinah Glory was all around me and in me, and that was my first encounter with the holy spirit! **Eugenia Gordon**

Testimony by Rev. Marcella Scott

Good morning Holy Spirit, I realize that You are on the inside of me, and that You are my leader and my guide. And if it had not been for You, living on the inside of me, I would not have made it this far, because the going can get pretty bad sometimes, But the God in me keeps me going through, cause victory is on the other side of through and after 49 years of being saved I am yet saved on today. And I celebrate being a Christiana and loving it more and more each and every day for Jesus Christ is Lord to the glory of God now and forever more and indeed so and amen to the Most High God and again amen. **Rev. Marcella Scott**

Testimony by Prophet Shirley E. Ford

My Relationship with the Holy Spirit is the most important relationship I have in my Life now that I am Enlighten with the evidence of HIS presence inside of me.

I depend on Him to lead me, to guide me and to strengthen me. The Holy Spirit is my consultant I partner up with Him daily that my day would be one of purpose. My Relationship with the Holy Spirit enables me to know when to speak and not to speak out of my emotions, prior to receiving the gift (the dwelling of the holy spirit) I had no control on the things I would say out of my mouth, with the Holy Spirit being my consultant it enables me to be quite or when to speak.

My relationship with the holy Spirit teaches me true humility, He weeps when he chooses, He is Bold, He is also Gentle as a lamb, my relationship with Him helps me realize I am nothing that is useable for Gods Glory and the people benefit without him. I am never alone; He is inside of me and wherever I am he is also; Truth is all He knows and with us being in a relationship I never have to worry about him lying to me. He gives me the strength to be true to myself. He is the only one that knows everything about me and still stay in the relationship. Whenever I need help, I can always count on Him, He is all anyone will ever need to help one live a life that will please God, and help you be the person God created one to be. **Prophet Shirley E. Ford**

Testimony by Elder Terrilyn Shorter

I remember my first encounter of the Holy Spirit that I was aware, and even today as I think about it, I stand in awe. I grew up as a Lutheran from a child up until about the age of 18. I would hear the preaching on the Trinity but never really knew the function, or that it was active or a live in me. I knew that I began to feel that I needed something more that some of the kids I had gone to school with services were different, more upbeat, more live music that seem to speak to what I called than was my insides, now I know it was the Spirit. I enjoyed it and got more out of it. So, I began to attend Baptist churches periodically. But fast forwarding unto my late twenties, I remember attending a revival with a friend of mine. Not really knowing what to expect, we had already said that we would leave by a certain time if they weren't finished. Well, let me tell you that was a life changing moment in my life. There were people dancing and talking in some dialect that I was not familiar with, but it was warming and soothing to me, and I began to feel an excitement on the inside. Before I knew it, I was up dancing around uncontrollable and could hear a dialect while I danced, praised and worshipped God. But I began to realize that the sound I heard was coming from me, and I couldn't stop it, nor could I stop praising! This went on for a few minutes and although the dancing and what I learned later the speaking in tongues had stopped, the Spirit of God was still on me. Needless to say, that we stayed the entire service, but what happened on the way home was even more overwhelming. While riding in the car I still felt the need to praise God. My girlfriend and I both were so high in the Spirit, that I remember telling her to stop the car I just want to get out and praise Him, I couldn't stop praising His name. Tears streaming down my face with tears of joy, fulfillment and peace that I hadn't experience before. I felt drunk without any alcohol. When I arrived at my house and got out of the car, I remember just yelling out Hallelujah, and Thank You Jesus! I got in my house and still was so high in the Spirit. My girlfriend called me when she got home, and we continued to talk about how we were feeling and what had happened. Well finally I went to bed, and it was late, but I remember wondering if I would still feel like this tomorrow. Well let me tell you when I woke up, that although I wasn't dancing around but I had the same joy, fulfillment and such a sweet peace.

But looking back now, I realize that the Spirit was with me all of the time. Speaking to me, directing me, encouraging me. What I learned later was that because I was never taught the role of the Holy Spirit in my earlier years in my Christian walk as my helper and as my keeper, that it was not just about speaking in tongues, and dancing. But that He was there every step of the way, every day of my life in my prayers, having me to pray for things and people I didn't know, giving me words to share with others, peace in the midst of chaos and turmoil in my life, directing me all along this journey of life. Hallelujah!!!!!!! Thank You Lord!!!!
Elder Terrilyn Shorter

<u>Testimony by Rev. Dr. Margo W. Williams</u>

Paul made this stark declaration: "I have discovered this principle of life—that when I want to do what is right, I inevitably do what is wrong (Romans 7:21)." He went on to say that the culprit of his repeated behavior/thoughts was due to evil. Many folks misuse this text as a basis to practice sin. Paul was bringing to our consciousness how much we need to depend on the power of the Holy Spirit to HELP us when we feel that we can't help ourselves. HOW do we do this? Glad you asked. ASK the Holy Spirit to HELP you desire and choose the righteous ways/path/choices. This is not magic; it is spiritual discipline. EVERY day it may require that you get on your knees and cry out to God and ASK Him to think through your mind, speak through your tongue, and live in your day! It is a mighty arrogant thing to trust that you (and me) have the power to live holy and righteous without His (God/Jesus/Holy Spirit) help. That same Paul preached: "...for in Him we live and move and have our being... (Acts 17:28).

Let's stop making excuses and pointing fingers at everybody else. Take a look at self. Be strong enough to ask the Lord to SEARCH you and HELP you!

Amen? **Rev. Dr. Margo W. Williams**

Testimony by Rev. Dr. Mary J. Bryant

As I, hungering and thirsting for more of Jesus, began to read and study my Bible, I came across Acts: Chapters One and Two. In those first two Chapters the Holy Spirit was given to the believers to be empowered to be a witness of Jesus Christ. They also spoke with other languages. Well, at that time, I was dealing with a challenging situation in my life. So, I was really pressing into God and trying to find a way out of that dark depressing place I was in before it completely consumed me. I needed help in an urgent and most critical way. When my eyes saw those verses, something on the inside of me came to life. At that moment, a change started happening in me like never before. My days and my nights were consumed with the Bible and the Holy Spirit. I needed to receive this promise Jesus talked about. At the time, I didn't hear any teachings about the Holy Spirit. So, the Bible was going to be my teacher. I prayed and prayed to have more of the Word of God taught to me. As I was going through the Bible, I was led to the Gospel of John and there I found even more about the Holy Spirit. Jesus said He would be a Comforter and the Teacher of all Truth (John 15:26-27; John 14:26). Now, I really became excited and very hopeful. These verses began my pursuit of the Holy Spirit. I truly believe that once I received the Holy Spirit, I would be taught the Word of God. So, I continued reading and studying my Bible. The Gospel of John helped me to understand being born again and I really started learning about repentance and salvation. I was at the point where I wasn't sure if I was saved yet. Yes, I was baptized in the name of the Father, Son and Holy Ghost and became a member of a church, but still wasn't sure. I was still searching for the evidence of my salvation. So, I prayed for God to give me the evidence of speaking in tongue. Not long after that prayer, I was stirred to open my mouth and speak. I opened my mouth, and these sounds came out I had never heard before. The more I allowed the Holy Spirit to speak through me, the stronger my faith became. That change in me continued. I experience an inward change to my heart. Peace became my companion and those dark depressing days lifted from me. To make a long story short, having the Holy Spirit as my Teacher was the beginning of a whole new life for me. He taught me things I wasn't hearing. He started teaching me about love, then forgiveness. He taught me about humility and giving. I can go on and on. My spirit was being fed with Spiritual food that I was craving. And this goes on to this very day and will continue on to the day of Jesus Christ. **Rev. Dr. Mary J. Bryant**

Five

~

Foreward

I met Dr. Mary Bryant several years ago at a conference where we were speakers. This meeting was powerful, and it was clear that God had purposed every detail. I was moved by Dr. Bryant's gentle spirit and sincere conviction for the Word of God. Her passion is expressed in her writings, as an accomplished author. Each book she has written has the common theme of spiritual development. This work, *Holy Spirit: The Promise, The Presence, The Power,* is her fifth publication. She is inviting her readers into an intimate study which is designed to forge deeper knowledge of our triune God and the person of the Holy Spirit.

Dr. Bryant is methodical in her approach because she wants the reader to understand who Holy Spirit is, what He does, and why we should acknowledge Him in our lives. In the same way that a master builder secures a strong foundation before constructing a house, Dr. Bryant lays a solid foundation for the reader to grow in his or her faith walk. She excavates the soil of your heart by digging in the Word to release the treasures of Scripture that will enlighten your understanding.

As a minister of the gospel, Dr. Bryant is well-suited to share about her knowledge of Holy Spirit and how He has made a difference in her life. As you get to know Him better, you will recognize how He has worked in your life already. Remember Jesus' words: "And I will pray the Father, and He will give you another Helper, that He may abide with you forever" (John 14:16 NKJV). We all need to know our constant companion, Holy Spirit.

Rev. Dr. Margo W. Williams
Graceful Fire Coaching
Margo W. Williams Ministries
Author of *Petty Pain: Understanding the Assignment of Offense*

Six

~

Introduction

The Holy Spirit – The Promise. The Presence. The Power. -- is my fifth inspirational book. My very first book is **Prayers, Poems, and Precious Moments**; followed by **I Recommend Jesus**; the next is **New Life in Christ by Faith** and the most recently published is **You Are God Alone**. I give God all the glory for allowing me to publish these books. I know without a doubt in my mind that if it wasn't for the grace of God, I could not produce these books. So, I thank Him and give Him all my devotion and adoration for considering me for this endeavor. I absolutely need Him every step of the way.

The Holy Spirit is one of the Godhead known as the Trinity or the eternal Triune God [God Father, God Son, God Holy Spirit]. Although, His full power and ministry was not revealed until Jesus ascended back to the Father, there are Old Testament passages that mentions Him and His work. In Genesis 1:2, we read about His active role in creation. Verse 2 states, "the Spirit of God was hovering over the waters". He was preparing for the creative word of God to shape the world. The Spirit is also the author of life. When God formed man from the dust, He breathed His Spirit into Adam's nostril, and he became a living soul (Genesis 2:7). Ever since God created time, we are introduced to the Spirit of God, who hovered over the earth. Every move of God we see the Spirit in partnership with the work of God. Every man and woman who were used by God has the power of the Holy Ghost to accomplish it.

Holy Spirit is God's personal presence with us and in us. He is like the very air in our lungs. Holy Spirit is the power of God in action. He exists in perfect harmony and unity with Father and Son. He is a person and not an "it" as some may think. Jesus said in John 14:16 the Father will send another Comforter like Him but in Spirit form. The Bible reveals that Holy Spirit is a person (Genesis 1:2; Job 33:4). Holy Spirit is Divine Person like the Father and the Son. We should not think of Him as just a mere influence or goose bumps. Holy Spirit has personal characteristics. Holy Spirit thinks (Romans 8:27), Holy Spirit feels (Romans 15:30), Holy Spirit wills (1st Corinthians 12:11), and Holy Spirit has the capacity to love and to enjoy fellowship. He is endorsed by Father and Son to bring believers into the intimate presence and fellowship of Jesus (John 14:16-18, 26). I know there are many arguments that Holy Spirit is not a person, but I believe that He is a person. I believe we should treat Holy Spirit as a person and regard Him as the infinite living God within our hearts, worthy to be worshiped, loved, and to be surrendered to. After all, He is continuing the work of Jesus Christ through Believers.

The one God exists in as three identifiable and distinct persons. They are not three gods, or three parts or expressions of God, but are three persons so completely united that they form the ONE True and Eternal God. God (Father), God (Son), God (Holy Spirit) were ever made or created, but exists equal in essential being, attributes, power and glory. I read somewhere that of the persons in the Trinity or Godhead none is God without the others and each with the others is God. All three Divine persons work in perfect unity that makes them one God.

As sinners who have fallen short of the glory of God, the first encounter we have with Holy Spirit is when our hearts have been convicted of sin (John 16:8). In my research, the Greek work for convict is "elencho". It means to convince someone of the truth; to reprove; to accuse, refute, or cross-examine a witness. In other words, Holy Spirit is like a prosecuting attorney who exposes evil, reproves evildoers, and convinces people that they are sinners and need a Savior. It is then, we are given the revelation that none of us can live up to the righteousness that God requires to be in His holy presence and the judgement that is coming to those who die without salvation (John 16:8-11). Once we repent (turn from our way to God's way) and by faith believe and receive what Jesus did for us, Holy Spirit regenerates us and now we are born-again, born from above, born of the Spirit and not of flesh. We now have a new nature and Holy Spirit helps us to live this new life successfully by the Word of God.

Unfortunately, many Christians don't really know what difference it would make if the Holy Spirit was not in the world. *"Christians today operate very little in the Holy Spirit because of their ignorance concerning the Holy Spirit himself."* – **Kathryn Kuhlman**. Therefore, it is with great sincerity that I have been inspired and led to write this book about Holy Spirit. If you haven't been thinking rightly about Holy Spirit, it is time to change your thinking. It is my personal revelation that no one will ever be able to know Jesus until they get to know Holy Spirit (John 16:13-15). *"The Holy Spirit is the greatest promoter who ever lived, and he promotes just one person: Jesus Christ."* – **Kathryn Kuhlman**. It is essential for ALL born-again believers to recognize the importance of the Holy Spirit in God's redemptive purpose. He is the seal of our salvation (Ephesians 1:13-14). The answers to the questions about how to be delivered from sin, how to live a balanced life under grace, and how to live the victorious Christian life comes through the ministry of Holy Spirit. Therefore, it is imperative that He is never grieved (Ephesians 4:30) or quench Him (1st Thessalonians 5:19).

Do you desire for Holy Spirit to have more of you-yet all of you? It is not that we get more of Holy Spirit, but He gets more of us. Do you sincerely desire to be controlled and empowered by Him? Then welcome Him and pursue Him! Make Holy Spirit your best friend. Yield yourself unto God as an instrument of righteousness (Romans 6:13). Present your body as a living sacrifice, holy, acceptable unto God (Romans 12:1).

So, as you read this book desire Him, open your heart and invite Holy Spirit to give you revelation light of the Will of God. Without Him we can never know Jesus Christ and without Jesus Christ we cannot know the Holy Spirit. If you have Christ, you have the Holy Spirit. **Selah.**

Seven

෨

Prayer

Father in Heaven, God of our Lord Jesus Christ and Father of glory, I pray that you give the person reading this book the Spirit of wisdom and revelation in the knowledge of Christ. I pray that the eyes of their understanding be enlightened; that they may know what is the hope of the Lord's calling and what are the riches of the glory of Christ's inheritance in the saints. I pray that they be strengthened with might through the Spirit in the inner man that Christ may dwell in their heart through faith and that they be rooted and grounded in love. I pray that s/he will comprehend with all the saints what is the width and length and depth and height to know the love of Christ which passes knowledge and s/he be filled with all the fullness of God (Ephesians 1:15-23; 3:14-19).

Father, thank You for the gift of Holy Spirit. Please teach Your children to hear His voice more clearly and to follow His leading in all that we do and speak. Help us to be aware of Him in every situation. Let Him be revealed to us in new and fresh ways.

Now to Him who is able to do exceedingly abundantly above all that we ask or think, according to the power that works in us, to Him be glory in the church by Christ Jesus to all generations, forever and ever. Amen. (Ephesians 3:202-21 KJV)

Eight

༄

The Promise. The Presence. The Power

The Holy Spirit is essential to the new life in Christ. He is the
Promise, the Presence and the Power of Believers.

The Promise.

God began making promises of the Holy Spirit long before Jesus came
in the flesh. It is seen throughout the Old Testament of the Holy Spirit
or Spirit of God. But for this book I want to use Jesus' teaching of the
promise of Holy Spirit. During Jesus' ministry, He spent a great deal of
time teaching His disciples in order to prepare them for the continuation
of His ministry. The promise of the Holy Spirit was an essential and
necessary part of their preparation. The promise of the Spirit doesn't
refer to the promise made by the Spirit but rather, to the Spirit as the
promise. After Jesus announced His departure, He also told the disciples
about another Comforter. "And I will pray the Father, and He shall give
you another Helper, that He may abide with you forever – the Spirit of
truth, whom the world cannot receive, because it neither sees Him nor
knows Him; but you know Him, for He dwells with you and will be

in you. (John 14:16-17). The Holy Spirit abides in those who actually know Jesus.

In Ephesians 1:13, He is called the Holy Spirit of Promise. "In whom ye also trusted, after that ye heard the word of truth, the gospel of your salvation: in whom also after that ye believed, ye were sealed with that Holy Spirit of Promise." He is God's all-inclusive promise for this Church Age. Jesus was adamant that His disciples tarry to receive this promise for the Holy Spirit (Acts 1:4-5). In order for the disciples then and now to carry on the work of Jesus Christ, they needed and need Holy Spirit (Acts 2:33). Soon after Jesus ascended, the disciples received the promise.

"And when the day of Pentecost was fully come, they were all with one accord in one place. And suddenly there came a sound from heaven as of a rushing mighty wind, and it filled all the house where they were sitting. And there appeared unto them cloven tongues like as of fire, and it sat upon each of them. And they were all filled with the Holy Ghost, and began to speak with other tongues, as the Spirit gave them utterance." Acts 2:1-4).

Jesus promised that He would send the Holy Spirit and as 120 of His disciples gathered together in prayer, they awaited the arrival of the Holy Spirit. They believed and they waited to receive the promise. Jesus knew He had to go back to heaven so that the Holy Spirit could be sent back for the disciples. The Holy Spirit is also for all believers who call on the name of the Lord and who the Lord shall call. The Spirit comes through faith (Galatians 3:14). Holy Spirit was promised as a permanent guide, teacher, seal of salvation, and comforter to the believers (John 14:16-18).

Hallelujah, we can now enjoy the promised blessing. We can receive the Spirit through faith, and we can enjoy the all-inclusive, life-giving Spirit by remaining in the authentic union with the Lord Jesus Christ day by day!

The Presence.

The Book of Acts records the events that took place on the Day of

Pentecost when the Holy Spirit comes, fulfilling Christ's promise to wait until the Holy Spirit comes to empower and direct the witness. The story in Acts is a very familiar passage. After Jesus' resurrection, He appeared to His disciples for forty days (1:3). He told them to wait in Jerusalem for the fulfillment of His promise concerning the Holy Spirit. Jesus told them that it was better for Him to go away and send the Holy Spirit to be with them than for Him to remain with them physically on earth. John 16:7 states, "Nevertheless, I tell you the truth: it is to your advantage that I go away, for if I do not go away, the Helper will not come to you. But If I go, I will send Him to you." Jesus was somewhat limited in His physical body while on earth. But Holy Spirit is not limited by time and space. He can dwell inside of every disciple of Jesus Christ every moment of every day. His presence is with of us and within us. His presence also brings the Father and the Son to dwell in us also (John 14:23). The presence of the Holy Spirit will bring the "greater works" Jesus talked about in John 14:12-14: Verily, verily, I say unto you, He that believeth on me, the works that I do shall he do also; and greater works than these shall he do, because I go unto my Father. Therefore, every born-again Believer is encouraged to cooperate in the work of the Holy Spirit.

The Power.

The Promise and the Presence bring the Power. Holy Spirit is the power of God. Jesus said in Acts 1:8, "But ye shall receive power, after that the Holy Ghost is come upon you: and ye shall be witnesses unto me both in Jerusalem, and in all Judaea, and in Samaria and unto the uttermost part of the earth." The disciples needed the power to be a witness of the resurrection of Christ to the world. This power wasn't just an ordinary power, but it was divine power. It was the Dunamis power of God Almighty. When the Holy Spirit descended upon believers at Pentecost, it was a powerful one. It was like the sound of "a rushing might wind". Some translation says, "a sound like the blowing of a violent wind". Acts 2:1-4 states that the presence of the promise of the Holy Spirit filled the room and tongues of fire that separated and came to rest on each of them.

All of them were filled with the Holy Spirit and began to speak in other tongues as the Spirit enabled them. The Holy Spirit's power was made manifest to a multitude of people on that day and 3,000 souls were saved. The power of the Holy Spirit was not designed solely for the first-century church. All born-again Believers are indwelt by the Spirit and thus have His power available (1st Corinthians 6:19).

His power leads us, convicts us, teaches us and equips us to do His work and spread the gospel. The Believer is given power to live the Christian life through the Spirit's power. Romans 8:13 states, "If ye through the Spirit do mortify the deeds of the body, ye shall live." It is "ye" who are to put to death the sinful deeds of the body, but you are to do it through the Spirit's power. When a new creature in Christ struggles in his own strength to live the Christian life, he will fail. It is by faith the power of the Holy Spirit must be appropriated daily (Romans 8:4-5). Jesus taught, "Deny yourself. Take up your cross and follow me." This means that the Believer trusts the Spirit to empower him. There is no special formula that makes the Spirit's power available. It is simply a reliance and surrender to Him. The Holy Spirit's powerful indwelling is an amazing gift we should never take lightly.

Nine

అలు

Holy Spirit - Get to Know Him

"The beginning of the True Christian life is to receive the Holy Spirit."
Andrew Murray

First and foremost, I believe Holy Spirit is a Person. The work of Holy Spirit can't be understood without first believing that He is a Divine Person, third Person in the Trinity with God Father and God Son. Holy Spirit is not just a Person, but He is God! As the God the Son is eternal, Holy Spirit is also eternal. He has existed forever (Hebrews 9:14). As the God the Father is everywhere, Holy Spirit is everywhere at once (Psalm 139:7). It is in this belief that Holy Spirit is worthy to receive our reverence, our adoration, our faith, our love, our obedience and our total submission and surrender.

I believe that one of the great errors in the minds of many Believers concerning Holy Spirit is that He is simply a principle or influence. However, Holy Spirit is not merely some mysterious influence to somehow get a hold of or "to catch". But He is infinitely holy, infinitely wise, infinitely mighty in power and infinitely kind and compassionate. It is the Holy Spirit who is to get hold of us and to use us according to His will. In other words, we don't say how can we get more of Him but instead we should say, "How can the Holy Spirit have more of me." We aren't in charge of the Holy Spirit; He oversees us. The more we yield and submit to Him the more of us He can use. I believe once we are totally surrendered to Holy Spirit, there is no limit to the availability and scope of His power in our life.

As a Divine Person of infinite majesty, Holy Spirit comes into our heart to make His dwelling and takes full possession of our life to make us a witness of Christ and to glorify God. I know when I give thought to this fact and truth that a person of Divine majesty and glory dwells in my heart and wants to use me, I become humbly overwhelmed with gratitude and honor.

Please understand that when I say Holy Spirit is a Person, I am not saying He has a physical body because He uses us as His body. But I am saying that He has all the distinctive characteristics or marks of personality. For example, knowledge, feelings, or emotion, and will is a person. All these characteristics of personality are ascribed to Holy Spirit in both the Old and New Testaments.

The best version of ourselves is always the new "man" and we live that life inside of Christ by the Holy Spirit. Becoming who we are created to be reveals itself when we walk in unity and oneness with the Holy Spirit. This is why we need to know Him. Because it is the Holy Spirit who leads us through this new life in Christ and reminds us of the Father's will and His word. For the born-again person, He has become our center of gravity and our guiding force for the new life – the transformed life. Giving us the Holy Spirit was an intentional and purposeful move by God the Father and the Son so we could be empowered with everything few could possibly need to be successful in please God and becoming like Christ Jesus. The Holy Spirit is given to be both in us and upon us. We should be eternally grateful for knowing our Counselor, Teacher, and Comforter. He is as close as our breath and will never depart from us (Isaiah 59:21; Hebrews 13:5).

Apostle Paul wrote in 1st Corinthians 2:10-11, "But God has revealed them to us through His Spirit. For the Spirit searches all things, yes, the deep things of God. For what man knows the things of a man except the spirit of the man which is in him? Even so no one knows the things of God except the Spirit of God (Holy Spirit) (NKJV). Here we can see Holy Spirit has knowledge. Clearly, Holy Spirit is more than an influence that illuminates our minds to comprehend the truth, but He knows the truth.

As a Person, Holy Spirit has a will. He is not a power we can catch and use according to our will. On the contrary, He is a Person of sovereign majesty who uses us according to His will. Read what 1st Corinthians 12:11 teaches, "But one and the same Spirit works all these things, distributing to each one individually as He wills." (NKJV). See it is by His will. Therefore, we must be obedient to Him. It is by the Spirit that we put to death the deeds of the body and live (Romans 8:14). It is by the Spirit that we will not gratify the desires of the flesh (Galatians 5:16). Having begun by the Spirit in our new birth, we are to live in obedience of the Spirit. We must believe and obey Him by faith which allows the life of Christ to be revealed in each of us. It is so important to get into a right relationship with Holy Spirit to know that He does not move by our will, but His sovereign will. We should all be so mindful and humbled that He is willing to dwell in us and take possession of us and use us according to His own perfect will. What an honor it is to be used by a Divine Person who never errs and is willing to take possession of us and impart His precious gifts and power as He wills.

We also learn about the mind of Holy Spirit as Apostle Paul wrote in Romans 8:27, "Now He who searches the hearts knows the mind of the Spirit is, because He makes intercession for the Saints according to the will of God." (NKJV). This word "mind" includes the ideas of thought, feeling and purpose. That is why we are told by Apostle Paul to be transformed by the renewing of our mind in Romans 12:2. A renewing of the mind involves repenting from our mind-set to that of Jesus Christ. Philippians 2:5 states, "Let this mind be in you, which was also in Christ Jesus." Holy Spirit helps us with this spiritual transformation. Colossians 3:1-2 teaches us this very important lesson for the born-again person, "If then you have been raised with Christ, seek the things that are above, where Christ is, seated at the right hand of God. Set your minds on things above not on things that are on earth." Then Romans 8:5b states, "For those who live according to the Spirit set their minds on the things of the Spirit." Holy Spirit enables us to know the mind of Christ according to the will of God. The Holy Spirit teaches comparing spiritual things with spiritual things (1st Corinthians 2:13-16).

It is Holy Spirit who "sheds God love in our hearts" (Romans 5:5). Just as we speak of the love of the Father and the Son, we should say that about Holy Spirit also. We teach and sing about the love of God and Jesus, but very seldom do we acknowledge the love of the Holy Spirit. It is also because of the love of Holy Spirit that He came into this world of sin and darkness to seek you and me out patiently purse us until we see our utter ruin and need for a Savior. He is the one that convicts the sinner's heart and reveals Jesus as Savior and Lord. Listen, if it had not been for the love of Holy Spirit, sent by the Father in answer to Jesus' prayer (John 14:16), I would still be "dead-man walking". It is because Holy Spirit who sought after me while I was in utter darkness and ruin. He pursued me even when I turned a deaf ear to His voice until finally, I listened, and He opened my eyes and my heart to see and heart that I was in a dead state, and I needed saving. He gave me the good news about Jesus Christ as Savior and Lord. Not only that Holy Spirit enable me to receive Jesus as my Savior and Lord. Hallelujah! If it was not for the love of Holy Spirit, I could have never; I would have never been born-again. I am so full of thanksgiving that He did not give up on pursing me. Oh, my brother and my sister get to know Holy Spirit on an intimate level. He is not just an influence, but He is a Divine Person just a real as God, Father and Son. So, you can rightly say, God loves me. Jesus loves me. Holy Spirit loves me.

Get to know Holy Spirit. He is the Spirit of Truth that guides us into all truth and show us the things of God to come; and God will be glorified (John 16:13-15). He will never fail us in the things of God. So, get to know Him that you will not grieve Him. Ephesians 4:30 states, "And grieve not the Holy Spirit of God, whereby you are sealed unto the day of redemption." In getting to know Holy Spirit you will find out that He sees clearly every act you perform, every word you speak, every thought you entertain, even idle thoughts you allow to go through your mind. Anything in act, word or deed that is impure, unholy, unkind, selfish, untrue, ungodly, or unrighteous will grieve Holy Spirit.

After Jesus ascended back to the Father, Holy Spirit was sent to be the Executor of the will and power of God. He is the Executor of the Godhead on Earth and in Lord in the Church. Holy Spirit is appointed to carry out every divine order of God. He can be known and experienced as Comforter, Counselor, Helper, Advocate, Intercessor, Strengthener, Keeper, Sustainer, Teacher, Revelator, Illuminator and Friend. Remember Jesus Himself placed a lot of emphasis on Holy Spirit. Jesus prayed to the Father to send another counselor to take His place on earth and in the church. Without the godly counsel of Holy Spirit, we will only have ungodly counsel of Satan. This is what John 14:16-17 state, "And I will ask the Father, and He will give you another Counselor to be with you forever. He is the Spirit of Truth. The world is unable to receive Him because it doesn't see Him or know Him, because He remains with you and will be in you." Holy Spirit is essential in the life of a Born-Again Believer! If Holy Spirit was essential for Jesus, the Only Begotten Son of God, He is essential for us as well. It is the communion with Holy Spirit that unites us with the grace of Jesus Christ and the love of God (2nd Corinthians 13:14).

On one of Apostle Paul's missionary assignments to Ephesus, he asked "certain disciples" if they had received the Holy Ghost since they believed. In other words, did you receive Jesus into your mind only or did you also embrace Him with your heart? Did He get inside of you? We you just immersed in water or were immersed into Jesus by faith? These disciples he was questioning were disciples of John the Baptizer. The answer him, "We have not so much as heard whether there be any Holy Ghost." (Acts 19:2). The baptism Paul was speaking about was not water baptism but being baptized into Jesus Christ. Too often we can get two mixed up. John's water baptism of repentance was an introduction or preparation for receiving Christ Jesus into their hearts. It was for them to be "enveloped" or "enclosed" with Jesus. Remember John the Baptizer's ministry was before Jesus was resurrected and ascended back to the Father. So, John's ministry was works. This what he said about his baptism in Luke 3:16, "I indeed baptize you with (into) water; but One mightier than I is coming, whose sandal strap I am not worthy to lose. He will baptize you with the Holy Spirit and fire." (NKJV). When we look at Acts 2:1-4, we see both the baptism of the Holy Ghost and the filling of the Holy Ghost.

Apostle Paul was speaking about a deeper level of salvation. He was talking about the word of faith. The Church quotes Romans 10:9 frequently and very loosely. "That if thou shalt confess with thy mouth the Lord Jesus, and shalt believe in thine heart that God hath raised Him form the dead, thou shat be saved." But failed to include Romans 10:10, "For with the heart man believeth unto righteousness; and with the mouth confession is made unto salvation." In other words, it is deeper than saying or repeating Romans 10:9. It involves repentance (a turning away and a turning to God [1 Timothy 2:5; Acts 26:20). It is acknowledging that Jesus came in the flesh (1 John 4:2), believing in the heart that God raised Him from the dead (Romans 8:11) and recognizing His power, authority, and majesty as God (Matthew 28:18) that is the person(s) who will be saved.

The Apostle knew that being filled with the Holy Ghost was essential for the disciples of John. After Paul informed them that John's baptism was one of repentance, telling the people to believe in Jesus, the Messiah and Savior, who was coming after him; they were baptized again – not with water- into the name of the Lord Jesus. Another water baptism wasn't necessary. Then Apostle Paul laid his hands upon them, and the Holy Ghost came on them; and the spoke with tongues and prophesied (Acts 19:5-6). When we are enveloped into Jesus, we received the in-dwelling of the Holy Spirit. Jesus said that who believes in Him from his innermost being will flow rivers of living water (John 7:38). Scripture teaches that He was speaking of the Holy Spirit. When Jesus said this, the Spirit had not yet been given because He was not yet glorified (John 7:39). Once those who believe in Him as Savior by faith, they receive the Holy Spirit afterward.

We must be a people who want to know the communion of the Holy

Spirit, the fellowship of the Holy Spirit, the partnership of the Holy Spirit. We must desire an intimate person friendship with the Holy Spirit. Why? Because Holy Spirit is the whole secret of a real and successful Christian life. The life of liberty, joy, power, peace, and fullness. For me personality, it is such a confidence to have Holy Spirit as my forever best friend to surrender my life to His control. I cannot live a godly life unless by the power of the Holy Spirit.

Listen, it is not enough to know the doctrine about this Divine Person, but you must know Holy Spirit for yourself. Therefore, as you read through this book on Holy Spirit, surrender to Him in every area of your life. He knows what's best for you me. He knows which way you and I need to take. Trust Him as the third Person of the Godhead with God Father and God Son. He is Lord over our spirit. I encourage each of you to make it your top priority to get to know Holy Spirit. You will never regret it! We cannot receive anything from God except through Holy Spirit. The Word has no power without the Holy Spirit. In other words, the Word has so little power to build up believers in holiness and in consecration because of the absence of the Holy Spirit. Selah. Therefore, it is absolutely essential that as a new creation in Christ, we must learn to allow Holy Spirit to cultivate a teachable spirit within us. We must allow Him to take complete ownership of this temple and not just be a guest. In fact, without Holy Spirit we cannot belong to Christ. It is through Holy Spirit that we are in union with Jesus Christ. Through Him we receive instructions, revelations and illumination in the heart that we may be conform to the image of Jesus Christ.

If Believers want to live a successful Christian life that is pleasing to God, it is imperative to learn to allow the Holy Spirit to cultivate a teachable spirit within them. As the Holy Spirit instructs Believers concerning God's Word, He will give revelation and illumination in their heart. Every Christian can and must live in the Spirit. This can only be realized as the Word of God is hidden in the heart.

My question to you today is are you living under the power of the Holy Spirit? Are you living an anointed, Spirit-filled and Spirit-led Christian life? And now are you willing to give yourself up to the Holy Spirit?

I encourage you to yield and surrender to Holy Spirit. May each of us continue to all the Holy Spirit to fill our heart with the truth of the Word of Christ for the glory of God (Colossians 3:16).

Ten

〜

Jesus and the Holy Spirit

"You, however, are not in the flesh but in the Spirit, if in fact the Spirit of God dwells in you. anyone who does not have the spirit of Christ does not belong to him."
Romans 8:9

In Genesis, God sets the stage for His plan of salvation. After the fall of the Adam and Eve, God promised that a descendant of Eve would crush the head of the serpent (3:15). God had an eternal plan to save those who were dead in their sins. Hebrews 10:5 states that God prepared a body for Jesus. In Luke's account of the gospel, we read about the angel Gabriel appearing to a young virgin named Mary. He told her that she would conceive and give birth to a son. When Mary inquired about how this would take place, Gabriel said, "The Holy Spirit will come on you, and the power of the Most High will overshadow you (1:26-38). So, when the time was right or in the "fullness of time" God sent His Son into the world as Savior (Galatians 4:4-5).

Then we read about the baptism of Jesus by John the Baptist. If you remember the story, when Jesus came up out of the water, the Holy Spirit descended in bodily form like a dove as the Father spoke (Luke 3:22). It was the Holy Spirit who led Jesus into the wilderness to be tempted by the devil (Luke 4:1-13). The Prophet Isaiah prophesied that the Spirit of the Lord would rest upon Him. Isaiah 11:1-5, "The Spirit of the LORD will rest on Him – the Spirit of wisdom and of understanding, the Spirit of counsel and of might, the Spirit of the knowledge and fear of the LORD"- This is the same life that comes to those who place their faith in His finished work. They could be born again by the power of the Holy Spirit and live in the power of the that same Spirit. Hallelujah!

After Jesus was baptized in the Jordan by John the Baptist, it was the Holy Spirit that led Him in the wilderness for 40 days without food or water to be tested by the Devil (Luke 4:1-13). Once Jesus came out of the wilderness, He returned to Galilee in the power of the Holy Spirit (Luke 4:14). He went into the synagogue and stood up to read the scroll of the prophet Isaiah that was handed to Him: The Spirit of the Lord is on me, because He has anointed me to proclaim good news to the poor, He has sent me to proclaim freedom for the prisoners and recovery of sight for the blind, to set the oppressed free, to proclaim the year of the Lord's favor (Luke 4:18-16). Some may think that because Jesus was God, His divine nature takes the place of His soul. However, this is not so. Remember Jesus came in the form of a human without the sin, but He was nonetheless a human. He experienced the same things weakness and was tempted in all things as we are (Philippians 2:7; Hebrews 4:15). Therefore, Jesus needed the Holy Spirit in order to have communion with God. He performed miracles in the power of the Holy Spirit (Matthew 12:18; Acts 10:38). Even Jesus' resurrection was carried out by the Holy Spirit (Romans 8:11). Jesus depended on Holy Spirit to be raised from the dead. Jesus was vindicated by His resurrection and through the Holy Spirit of Holiness Jesus "was declared with power to be the Son of God" (Romans 1:3-4). Jesus had a very special relationship with Holy Spirit. According to Christ's human nature, He exercised faith, love, reverence, humility, obedience and the graces proper to a true human nature in the power of the Holy Spirit. In other words, a true and proper human being is realized only in communion with God.

Jesus was God (John 1:1), but He was also human (1ˢᵗ Titus 2:5). Therefore, as a human He needed the Holy Spirit to empower Him for

His earthly ministry. Jesus knew He was anointed to fulfill the will of the Father. In other words, Jesus was the God-Man who could live, serve and proclaim the gospel only as a Spirit-anointed man. Acts 10:38 teaches that God anointed Jesus with the Holy Spirit and with power and He went about doing good and healing all that were oppressed of the devil because God was with Him. All that Jesus did in His earthly ministry was because of anointing of the Holy Spirit. The Holy Spirit remained on Jesus throughout His stay on earth. Then at His ascension back to the Right Hand of the Father, He received the Holy Spirit from the Father and poured Him out on His people at Pentecost (Acts 2:33; Jon 16:5-14). This also confirmed His Lordship as Prophet, Priest, and King in His exalted position. The Holy Spirit testifies to the exalted Savior's continual presence and authority.

Jesus stood up at the last and greatest day of the festival and shouted that if anyone who was thirsty, they could come to Him and drink. But the only way they could receive this water was to believe in Him (John 7:37). Jesus was speaking of the Holy Spirit who was not given yet because He was not yet glorified (John 7:39). Before Jesus went to the cross, He encouraged His disciples with deep spiritual realties about the Father and the Holy Spirit. In John 14:15-17, He said, "If you love me, keep my commands. And I will ask the Father, and he will give you another advocate to help you and be with you forever – the Spirit of Truth." Though the disciples didn't fully understand, Jesus assured them that He would not leave them as orphans. (John 14:18-20). Once Jesus breathed on the disciples, an impartation of the Holy Spirit was given (John 20:22). This was the disciples' initial new covenant experience of the regenerating presence of the Holy Spirit and the impartation of new life from the risen Christ, who was now glorified. This was not a symbolic prophecy of the outpouring on the day of Pentecost. Both the receiving of the Spirit and the baptism of the Spirit were both needed by the disciples. Jesus told them in John 15, "When the Advocate comes, whom I will send to you from the Father – the Spirit of Truth who goes out from the Father - He will testify about Me. And you also must testify, for you have been with me from the beginning (vv. 26:27). Then He continued, "But when He, the Spirit of Truth, comes, He will guide you into all the truth. He will not speak on His own; He will speak only what He hears, and HE will tell you what is to yet to come. He will glorify Me because it is from me that He will receive what He will make know to you. All that belongs to the Father is mine. That is why I said the Spirit will receive from Me that He will make known to you." Like the first disciples, we also need the indwelling and the outpouring of the Spirit of God to carry out this great commission given in Matthew 28:18-20 and to perform miracles, signs and wonders.

This is where we find Jesus giving the disciples instructions to wait in Jerusalem until the Holy Spirit came upon them (Acts 1:4-5). Jesus Himself baptized them in the Holy Spirit (John 1:33). The disciples needed this fire baptism because this would be the sign and dynamic mark of the followers of Jesus. The Holy Spirit was poured out on them so that they might carry on and carry out the work of Christ in the world. The Holy Spirit is the power they received. I believe "you will receive power" is the key verse in the book of Acts. This power is more than strength or ability; it is power in operation or in action. Please note the baptism in the [Holy] Spirit does pertain to a personal salvation and regeneration, but to the power of a believer to witness with great effect. It is receiving the power to witness for Jesus Christ so that those who are separated from God can be reconciled back to Him and to teach them to obey all that Christ Jesus commanded (Matthew 28:18-20; Luke 24:49; John 15:26-27; Acts 1:8). Christ is made known, loved, praised and made Lord of God's chosen people.

This power is sometimes referred to as Dunamis power. In Luke's account of the Gospel and in the Book of Acts, he emphasizes the power of Holy Spirit included the authority to drive out evil spirits and the anointing to heal the sick (Luke 4:14, 18, 36; 5:17; 6:19; 9:1-2; Acts 6:8; 8:4-8, 12-13; 10:38; 14:3; 19:8-12). The disciples were empowered by the Holy Spirit that caused them to witness "with great boldness" (Acts 29), "with great power...to testify" (4:33), with "many" signs, wonders and miracles (2:43; 5:12-16; 6:8; 8:6-8; 14:3; 19:11-12), and with great results (4:4; 6:7; 8:8; 9:33-35; 11:21,24; 12:24; 14:21; 16:5; 19:10,20). Just as

Jesus Christ was anointed and fitted for service by the Holy Spirit, so does all Believers. Jesus with the anointing of the Holy Spirit carried out everything the Father gave Him to do here on earth. That is why He could say, "It is Finished."

Jesus knew how important the disciples of then and now needed and need the Holy Spirit for this new life. It is in John 14:26, Jesus told His disciples, "But the Comforter, which is the Holy Ghost, whom the Father will send in My name, He shall teach you all things, and bring all things to your remembrance, whatsoever I have said unto you." The Holy Spirit is also the Spirit of Truth, and He testifies of Jesus (John 15:26). Let me mention how serious Jesus is about Holy Spirit. He warned the disciples not to blasphemy the Holy Spirit. Jesus warned that anyone who did so would not be forgiven (Matthew 12:31-32; Mark 3:29; Luke 12:10). Jesus prepared His disciples for His departure by promising them another Helper, Teacher, and Comforter. Through Holy Spirit Jesus would continue to be with them and Christ would be glorified. This is the main mission of Holy Spirit (John 16:14). Just as the Son was enabled by Holy Spirit to glorify the Father, so all believers to glorify both the Son and the Father. It is important to understand that the Holy Spirit's work in believers begins and ends with the revelation that we are here on earth to glorify the Son and the Father by the power of the [Holy] Spirit.

Jesus is still saying, "If anyone is thirsty, let them come to me and drink" (John 7:37). He is saying to ask, and it will be given to you, seek and you will find and knock, and the door will be opened to you (Matthew 7:7-12, Luke 11:5-13). The Holy Spirit is only given by faith in Jesus. No one can work for this precious gift of grace. Galatians 3:14 teaches, "That the blessing of Abraham might come on the Gentiles through Jesus Christ; that we might receive the promise of the [Holy] Spirit through faith."

The work of the Holy Spirit in Christ Ministry

- Christ conceived by Him according to Luke 1:35
- Christ performed miracles by Him according to Matthew 12:28

- Christ was anointed by Him according to Matthew 3:16
- Christ was supported by Him according to Luke 4:1, 17, 18
- Christ was filled by Him according to Luke 4:1
- Christ was offered to God by Him according to Hebrews 9:14
- Christ was raised by Him according to Romans 1:4
- Christ was justified by Him according to 1st Timothy 3:16

Eleven

༄

The Three Cs of the Holy Spirit:

Conviction. Conversion. Consecration.

Conviction

> *"And when He [Holy Spirit] comes He will convict the world of its sin..."* John 16:8 NLT

Conviction is the work of the Holy Spirit where a person is able to see himself as God sees him: guilty, defiled, and totally unable to save himself. (https://carm.org/dictionary/conviction)

Jesus said that when Holy Spirit comes, He will convict the world of sin, of righteousness, and of judgement. John 16:8 states, "And when He is come, He will reprove the world of sin, and of righteousness, and of judgment (KJV). He convicts the world of sin because they do not believe in Jesus, of righteousness because Jesus is with the Father and of judgment because the ruler of this world is judged (John 16:9-11). The Holy Spirit exposes sin and unbelief in order to awaken a consciousness of guilt and need for forgiveness. Holy Spirit convinces people that Jesus is the righteous Son of God, resurrected, vindicated and now the Lord of lords and King of kings. Holy Spirit makes people award of God's standard of righteousness in Christ Jesus. Holy Spirit doesn't just show them what sin is, but He gives them power to overcome the world.

Since the fall of man in the Garden, this world is a sinful place. There is only one way humanity can know of their sinful condition and that is by the Holy Spirit. Unless the Holy Spirit is at work in a sinner's heart to convict of sin, no amount of preaching, pleading, or condemning will bring about conviction. The basic sin is unbelief or a refusal to trust in Jesus Christ as Messiah. This is the primary job of the Holy Spirit in the convicting of sin.

Conviction deals with the heart attitude of not trusting and believing Jesus. In the church, we quote Romans 10:9, "That if thou shalt confess with thy mouth the Lord Jesus, and shalt believe in thine heart that God hath raised him from the dead, thou shalt be saved." Here is where teaching comes into play. Because we must expound on verse 9 by teaching verse 10, "For with the heart man believeth unto righteousness; and with the mouth confession is made unto salvation." Though we are presented with God's initiative in grace and the humble obedience to it, it must be applied to the truth of the gospel of Christ. In other words, a person is not saved by confession of the mouth, but rather, the mouth testifies readily of the grace of God in Christ which has to be received by faith. It is in the heart that we believe. Therefore, it is the heart that has to be circumcised, made new. It is the heart that has to be circumcised and it is Holy Spirit who cuts away the old nature through sanctification. When a person receives conviction by Holy Spirit, the Good News of Jesus becomes more than facts to be believed. It is now a life of righteousness to be lived as new creations justified freely by God's grace through the redemption that is in Christ Jesus. Now the believer's relationship to sin, their position, is that they are dead to the principle of sin (Romans 6:1-14) and the practice of sin (Romans 6:15-23). It is the work of Holy Spirit that indwells and empowers every believer to accomplish this. For without the power of Holy Spirit it would be impossible in our strength to overcome sin and the power of sin. However, we MUST cooperate with Him in this process. The conviction of the Holy Spirit in an unsaved person's life will lead that person to the revelation that he is guilty, that

God is just, and that all sinners are deserving of God's judgment and wrath. Through the Holy Spirit, it is made known that no one is too far gone for Jesus to save them.

The gift of God's righteousness follows this conviction which is received by everyone who comes to Christ by faith. Apostle Paul wrote in Romans 1:17, "For therein is the righteousness of God revealed from faith to faith". I believe this means that we start by faith, we continue by faith, and we end by faith. In other words, start with Jesus, stay with Jesus, and end with Jesus. Apostle Paul has been uniquely given the grace to encourage and equip all saints as well as to challenge them spiritually. Everything he has suffered and have been enabled to accomplish for Christ Jesus gives him a sure foundation from which to draw as it helps them in their trials, test and spiritual growth. He lets every believer know that the righteousness from God is revealed from first to last – from the first faith for salvation to the last faith that is the salvation of our souls, which is the goal of our faith (1st Peter 1:9). Remember, salvation is not only the rescue from sin, but it is also rescue from the justified punishment of God. This is the rescue that comes through faith in the finished work of Jesus through His crucifixion, His resurrection, and His ascension which completely and perfectly erases the eternal separation between a holy God and imperfect humanity. Ultimately, those who come to Jesus in faith and trust are saved to the great glory of God. And Holy Spirit causes the conviction to get it all started.

So, the basis of salvation is God's gracious provision (Romans 3:23-26). Therefore, the only way a sinner can appropriate this gift of salvation is by faith. Paul reminds us that the just shall live by faith and the only way we can be justified is by faith in Jesus; if we believe that "There is one God and one Mediator who can reconcile God and humanity—the man Christ Jesus. He gave his life to purchase freedom for everyone." (1st Timothy 2:5-6 NLT). And when we believe this, the Boob of Acts 3:19 states, "Now repent of your sins and turn to God, so that your sins may be wiped away. Good News, we have life or union with God but if we don't then we have death or separation from God. We must first have *saving faith* which is trusting in Christ and Him alone for salvation (Acts 16:31). We then must have *justifying faith* which is our reliance on the fact that God has declared us righteous at the moment of salvation (Romans 3:21-26; 5:1). In other words, Justification does not make us righteous, but it pronounces us righteous. Justification comes from placing our faith in the finished work of Jesus Christ. It is the sacrificial death and the outpouring of His Blood that we are justified, and it allows God to see us as perfect, holy and without blemish in Christ (2nd Corinthians 5:21; 2nd Corinthians 5:17; Romans 8:30). As Believers in Christ, God sees Christ own righteousness when He looks at us. *In 2nd Corinthians 5:21* it states: "For our sake he made him to be sin who knew no sin, so that in him we might become the righteousness of God." (English Standard Version).

Concerning judgment, the Holy Spirit convinces people that Satan was defeated at the Cross (John 12:31; John 16:11), God's present judgement of the world (Romans 1:18-32) and the future judgment of the human race (Matthew 16:27; Acts 17:31; Acts 24:25; Romans 14:10; 1st Corinthians 6:2; 2nd Corinthians 5:10; Jude 14). The bible teaches that there is a day of judgement that is going to take place. That day will be where a holy God mete out justice and rid this world of sin. And that judgement has already begun at the finished work on the Cross. Jesus stated that Satan was the one on whom judgement fell. In John 12:31 He stated, "Now is the judgment of this world; now will the ruler of this world be cast out." We know that it was on the Cross that Christ redeemed sinners for God and utterly drove out Satan. Therefore, Jesus Christ death on the Cross broke the power of him who held the power of death (Hebrews 2:14). Jesus' resurrection shows and proves that Satan's rule has been overthrown. Christ announced to His disciples in Matthew 28:18 "All authority (all power of absolute rule) in heaven and on earth has been given to Me." (AMP). Ephesians 1:21 teaches, "...which He exerted when He raised Christ from the dead and seated Him at the right hand in the heavenly realms, far above all rule and authority, power and dominion, and every name that is invoked, not only in the present age but also the one to come. (NIV). Remember all who does not accept Christ and remain in their sin will be condemned along with Satan, and this is the warning Holy Spirit seeks to convict the unsaved of before it is too late.

The ministry of Holy Spirit in the conviction of sins is also for the Believers to teach, correct, and guide them into the truth (John 16:13; Matthew 18:15; 1 Timothy 5:20; Revelation 3:19). He works in Believers to reproduce Jesus holy life in their lives and Christ is formed in them (Galatians 4:19). Believers who God foreknew, He also predestined to be conformed to the image of His Son (Romans 8:29). Therefore, if the Believer ignores or rejects the convicting work of the Holy Spirit, they will enter into condemnation. Sin is a destructive force that destroys both the life and fullness of the Holy Spirit within the Believer (Romans 6:23, Romans 8:13; Galatians 5:17).

Holy Spirit comes to reveal sin, teach people the ways of God's righteousness and of judgement. He is God's means of communication on earth. Holy Spirit instructs Believers and leads them to follow the plans, purpose, wisdom and will of God. Holy Spirit as the Counselor is the reminder of Jesus and His ministry. He continues where Jesus left off in the earth. Holy Spirit's greatest work is to testify of Jesus. He works through Believers to accomplish God's purposes and reveal His power over the powers of darkness and His power to convince people to believe (John 12:28-50). May we all surrender to the ministry of Holy Spirit like never before.

Conversion

> *"And said, Verily I say unto you, Except ye be converted, and become as little children, ye shall not enter into the Kingdom of Heaven."*
> **Matthew 18:3 KJV**

Conversion is the turning of a sinner from sin to God

When Jesus said to the disciples *"be converted"*, He was essentially saying to them "to turn". Conversion is a "turning" from sin and of one's whole life and person towards God. It is more than mental acknowledgement of the truth or intellectual knowledge, but it is to become as little children; to be born-again (converted) as a spiritual infant, characterized by faith and humility. And we know that this is absolutely necessary to enter into the Kingdom of Heaven. I like the way the Passion Translation states this verse: "Learn this well: Unless you dramatically change your way of thinking and become teachable, and learn about heaven's kingdom realm with the wide-eyed wonder of a child, you will never be able to enter in." Remember when Jesus was speaking with Nicodemus, a prominent religious leader, saying that the only way to see and enter into the Kingdom was to be born-again of water and Spirit (John 3:6). It takes faith to be born-again. Apostle Paul taught in Acts 20:21 to turn to God and put faith in the Lord Jesus; for there is only One Mediator between God and humanity and that is Jesus (1st Timothy 2:5). In the Bible faith is presented as an absolute necessity for salvation. In fact, we cannot please God without faith (Hebrews 11:6).

I believe all conversion is started, continued, and finished by the power of Holy Spirit. The Holy Spirit converts men through the revealed and written Word of God. It is a conversion from the old life to the new life. We must understand that true conversion involves changing direction. It is turning from one thing to another. The true spiritual conversion radically alters the direction of a person's life. Please let me stress that this is not a partial change. You can't be born-again and still keep the old self. You can't straddle the fence. You can't have one foot in the Kingdom and one foot in the world. Conversion is not a superficial and shallow turning. Holy Spirit just doesn't rearrange the outward behavior of a person's life. Unlike sanctification, conversion is not a gradual change that occurs over a period of time. Therefore, conversion occurs at a much deeper level in a person. The person makes a decision to turn away from old patterns of sin and the world and turn towards God embracing the new life in Christ by faith.

My conversion by and with Holy Spirit was so profound and radical. Once I was convicted and converted, my mind changed about myself, sin, and Christ. I saw God like never before. I was overwhelmingly sorrowful for sinning against God. I wept and still weep at the goodness of God. Everything I knew changed radically! It wasn't a problem for me to change my will, but it was intentional, turning away from the direction that I was going in and turning to God and His way. In other words, conversion is the entire person, mind, heart, and will, is radically, completely, and fully changed. Being Born-again or regeneration and conversion should go hand in hand sort of speak. Regeneration is the cause, and conversation is the effect. I once read that regeneration is the root and conversion are the fruit.

I truly believe that some who are born-again fail to turn and be converted. I believe Apostle Paul wrote in his letter to the Corinthians about those who aren't converted. He essentially said that he couldn't talk to them as to spiritual people, only as people who are worldly because they were dominated by the earthly nature. I believe the apostle called them mere infants. In other words, they were unspiritual and unchanged by faith (1ˢᵗ Corinthians 3:1-4). There has to be conversion with the born-again experience. When there is a true conversion, a person will not remain carnal. It is impossible for a person to come to faith in Christ Jesus and then proceed to live their life in a carnal manner, with no evidence of being born again or a new creation (2ⁿᵈ Corinthians 5:17). This is absolutely unscriptural because the bible makes this abundantly clear that genuine faith will always inspire action. Faith without works cannot be called faith. Faith that doesn't produce is a dead faith (James 2:17). Faith must be visible. Faith is not just saying words, but it produces doers because it obeys the Word of God. In other words, it is demonstrated by obedience. Yes, faith is essential in conversion. We choose wisdom from heaven and reject earthly wisdom by faith. Simply put, faith produces separation from the world and submission to God.

Once we are convicted, conversion should follow, and we should pursue maturity from there. Here's the thing, in saving us, God desires that we grow in grace and in the knowledge of Christ, our Lord (2ⁿᵈ Peter 3:18). He desires for Christ to be formed in as the new man. We do this by doing what Apostle Paul commands in Romans 12:1-2. We are to present our bodies as a living sacrifice, not being conformed to this world but being transformed into the image and likeness of Christ by the renewing of our mind. In other words, we are to be increasing spiritually and decreasing carnally. This process is sanctification. It is by the sanctifying work of Holy Spirit. He plays a vital role in our conversion process more than is taught in the church.

Holy Spirit is God's transforming power for the converted believer (Romans 8:13-14). Why is this so important? Because it is impossible for anyone to overcome sin without His help. We must surrender our life to God and receive the gift of Holy Spirit. It is those who are led by the Spirit of God that are sons of God. In other words, those who are led by the Spirit of God has the nature and character of God. Remember Colossians 1:27 teaches that Christ lives in us. It is by the yielding to the power and leading of Holy Spirit that we allow Christ to live actively in us. It is by partnering with Holy Spirit that we can succeed at living a converted life.

It is through this transformation Believers can imitate Christ in their thoughts, attitudes, and actions. We must purposefully and intentionally allow the work of Holy Spirit to become the leading force in our lives to produce the qualities of a true disciple. God does not want His children to remain infants and carnal minded but be transformed by the renewing of the mind (Romans 12:2). Discipleship is a lifetime of overcoming and growing; of transforming our thoughts and mind to become like Jesus (Philippians 2:5). Jesus instructs His disciples to deny themselves, take up their cross and follow Him. With the Holy Spirit we can join in with Philippians 4:13, "I can do all things through Christ who strengthens me." Our conversion makes God our focus, Jesus Christ our glory and Holy Spirit our life.

Consecration

"Who have been chosen according to the foreknowledge of God the Father, through the sanctifying work of the Spirit, for obedience

to Jesus Christ and sprinkling by His blood: Grace and peace be yours in abundance."
1st Peter 1:2

Consecration is to regard as set apart or separate (https://biblestudy-tools.com/dictionary/consecrate/)

Leviticus 20:7 states, "You shall consecrate yourself therefore and be holy, for I am the Lord your God." We see that even in the Old Testament that God's people were called to holy, different and separated from all other people in order to belong to God as His very own. In the New Testament, God also calls Believers to be separate from the corrupt world system and from unholy compromise (John 17:15-16; 2nd Timothy 3:1-5). In essence, consecration means set apart from evil, set apart to God and be prepared to be used for the glory of God. Sanctification is also another word for consecration. So, I will use them interchangeably.

There can be no reconciliation without cleansing. Thus, there is no consecrating without cleansing. To cleanse is to separate from sin but to sanctify or consecrate is to separate to God. It is to set apart to God what has already been separated from sin. Trying to set apart something that isn't cleansed is like dressing a pig in a clean garment. In other words, you can't set apart to a holy use that which is not clean. It was said by Dr. Chalmers that in conversion, God gives to us, but in consecration we give to God. Therefore, in consecration, we surrender ourselves to God. Apostle Paul states it best in Romans: I beseech you therefore, brethren, by the mercies of God, that you present your bodies a living sacrifice, holy, acceptable unto God, which your reasonable service. (12:1). This means nothing is held back from God. There is a transference of ownership. We have to see ourselves as the absolute property of God. "For you were bought at a price; therefore, glorify God in your body and in your spirit, which are God's (1st Corinthians 6:20 NKJV). Now it becomes our will for God's will.

Notice in Apostle Peter's first letter in chapter one and verse two, the work of Holy Spirit in the sanctifying work. The converted person should live a set apart life that reflects the nature of God (1st Peter 1:16). There must be a right relationship with Holy Spirit in this consecrated process. I believe the first step is to believe that there has been a change from sinner to saint. Some have a problem with this truth. But the bible tells us that we are called to be saints (1st Corinthians 1:2) set apart to God for His Kingdom. Remember Born-again Believers are new creations, totally new in the world, which Holy Spirit rules (Romans 8:14; Galatians 5:25). As saints, new creations, we are renewed after God's image (Colossians 3:10), sharing His glory (2nd Corinthians 3:18) with a renewed knowledge and understanding, and living a life of holiness (Ephesians 4:24). It is the Holy Spirit who directly communicates the realities of God. It is only through Holy Spirit that we begin to receive and understand spiritual realities.

Consecration is not a one-time act, but it is continuous. In fact, consecration has a very important role in our maturity towards God. However, there is a partnership that has to take place. We have to partner with Holy Spirit. On our part we must separate ourselves from what is contrary to God. We must "put off the old and put on the new" (Colossians 3:10). This is called repentance. Then Holy Spirit prepares us to be used by actually making us holy. Ephesians 2:10 informs us that we are God's masterpiece, and He has created us new in Christ Jesus for the good works that He has planned from the before time began. In being prepared for the good works, our bodies will need to be cleansed. The work on the inside has to now work on the outside. In other words, as we draw near to God, He draws near to us. We decrease so that He will increase. When Jesus said that to be His disciples, a person must deny themselves, pick up his/her cross and follow Him. This is a great example of our part in consecration. This is a daily process. Consecration has to become a way of life. Let me note here that in the New Testament, the sanctification picture is not a slow process of forsaking sin little by little. But it shows a definitive act by which the saint by grace is set free from Satan's bondage and makes a clear break with sin in order to live for God. Romans 6:18 clearly states that we have been set free from the bondage sin and became salves to righteousness. Saints must live as those made alive in Christ which is what consecration really is. Consecration is the path in which God is glorified with our life, from the inside out. Both our condition and position have been exchanged and changed. "Since, then, you have been raised with Christ, set your hearts on things above, where Christ is, seated at the right hand of God. Set your minds on things above, not on earthly things. For you died, and your life is now hidden with Christ in God." (Colossians 3:1-3). The Bible commands saints to put to death their earthly nature (Colossians 3:5). Again, consecration is a lifelong process in which we continue to put to death the misdeeds of the body (Romans 8:1-17) to progressively be transformed into Christ likeness (2nd Corinthians 3:18). We continue to grow in grace and in the knowledge of our Lord (2nd Peter 3:18). Thank God for Holy Spirit who enables us through this process.

Therefore, once Christ has sanctified the heart (1st Peter 3:15), we present ourselves to God through Holy Spirit. Christ has to not just be the Savior, but He must also be Lord. A consecrated or sanctified life is a Christ-centered life, and a Christ-centered life is a Spirit-led life. When this is the case, Jesus is magnified, and God is glorified in our life. The Holy Spirit is essential in becoming consecrated. It is the Holy Spirit that makes us effective in pointing people to Christ. This is why the Bible tells us not to grieve (Ephesians 4:30) or quench (1st Thessalonians 5:19) the Spirit. We need Him for this new life of consecration where Jesus is Lord. So, present your bodies a living sacrifice, holy, well pleasing to God, which is your reasonable service (Romans 12:1).

Simply put, Jesus purchased us with His own blood, and we belong to Him. We give ourselves to the Lord by partnering with Holy Spirit. We participate in His sanctifying work. We are set apart from sin and set apart to God to have intimate fellowship with God and serve Him with gladness. It is time to come out from among them (this world system, every evil and wicked way, every ungodly counsel, ungodly ties, etc.) and be separated unto God's way (the Kingdom realm, under the rule, reign, and royalty of God) to advance His Kingdom and Kingdom agenda. The consecration process is the door we enter through to be joined as one with the Father and the Son by the Holy Spirit. Each of us have to make the decision to grow from glory to glory in the Lord. Holy Spirit is the gateway to the God the Father and God the Son.

Twelve

༄

The Holy Spirit and Salvation

"Not by works of righteousness when we have done, but according to His mercy He saved us, by the washing of regeneration, and renewing of the Holy Ghost;"
Titus 3:5

Salvation – The deliverance, by the grace of God, from eternal punishment for sin which is granted to those who accept by faith God's conditions of repentance and faith in the Lord Jesus. Salvation means death to and freedom from sin (Romans 6), a new perspective that transcends the human point of view and participation in a new creation (Romans 5:16-17), peace with God (Romans 5:1), life as adopted children of God's (Galatians 4:4), baptism into Christ's death (Romans 6:4), and the reception of the Holy Spirit (Romans 5;8)

Salvation is the way into a new and secure relationship with God through the Blood of Jesus and is implemented, affirmed, and guaranteed (sealed) by Holy Spirit. As displayed in Titus 3:5, Holy Spirit has an essential and indispensable role in our salvation. It is not automatic that we belong to God just because He so loved the world, He sent His Only Begotten Son to take on the judgement of the world. Nor does the Son automatically saves us just because of His finished work. But there are

51

three wonderful works (restraining, convicting, and regenerating) performed by Holy Spirit in preparing unsaved people to become Born again Believers. Salvation is not accomplished by works of self-righteousness, but according to God's mercy by the washing of regeneration and the renewing of the Holy Spirit, that results in being born again (John 3:3). Please note that this not a reference to water baptism but to the spiritual renewing produced by the Holy Spirt. Consequently, we are justified by Grace. Therefore, without the ministry of God the Holy Spirit in and on us we would not benefit from the love of God the Father or from the sacrifice of God the Son.

In His ministry, Holy Spirit prepares the lost to become Born again by restraining the evil one. He lifts a standard against the enemy of our souls. Yes, Satan would like nothing more than to destroy the unsaved before they have a chance to choose to accept Jesus as Savior and Lord. Apostle Paul wrote, "The god of this age has blinded the minds of unbelievers, so that they cannot see the light of the gospel that displays the glory of Christ, who is the image of God. (2nd Corinthians 4:4 (NIV). God made Jesus who had no sin to be sin for us, so that in Christ, we might become the righteousness of God (2nd Corinthians 5:21). This is what Satan is trying to do. So, Holy Spirit causes conviction of sin and unrighteousness. In Hebrews it is Holy Spirit who says: Today, if you hear my voice hardened not your heart. God the Father draws us to Jesus (John 6:44) by the Holy Spirit to receive salvation. He gives us faith to see what Jesus did on our behalf. He makes Christ present in our hearts. Holy Spirit moves differently from person to person. He knows how, when and what it will take for a person to repent and surrender. He helps us to see our sins and current condition to confess and repent. However, the Holy Spirit will not override our will.

Through the regeneration (new nature) the ministry of Holy Spirit begins the process of making us complete in Jesus Christ and be successful in our walk as Believers, maturing in the knowledge of God our Lord Jesus Christ. He brings us in union with Christ. Salvation cannot happen without being born again and we cannot be born again except through the Holy Spirit. The Holy Spirit takes the Word of God, the Word of

Truth, and plants it in the heart of the sinner whom He will save; and that seed, that Word, watered and nurtured by the Holy Spirit, springs up into eternal life. The work in the heart of people is performed by the Holy Spirit in His own way and in His own time.

Salvation is the most common expression in the Bible used to identify the subjective changes in people's lives, when by faith they have received the benefit of Christ's death and resurrection. It implies deliverance, safety, preservation, healing, and soundness. It is recorded in scripture in three phrases. First, the Christian has been saved from the guilt and penalty of sin (Ephesians 2:5, 8). Second, the Christian is being saved from the habit and dominion of sin in this life (Galatians 2:19-20; 1st Corinthians 1:18) Third, when the Lord returns, the Christian will be saved from all the physical results of sin and of God's curse on the world (Romans 8:18-23; Hebrews 9:28). Salvation is completely from God. Saving faith is man's doing his part in response to God's having done His part. There is no other way to be saved but by the explicit gospel of Christ, the power of God unto salvation (Romans 1:16-17). Jesus said in John 14:6, "I am the way, the truth, and the life. No one comes to the Father except through Me." And the Father does the drawing [by the Holy Spirit]. We can't be saved any other way.

I had a very interesting salvation journey. I believe that process started before time began, spiritually speaking. But I can remember when I was a little girl. I would go in the "front room" (living room) when no one else was around and I would take the family Bible from the mantle above the fireplace just to flip through the pages. I remember the scent of those pages as my little fingers flipped through them. I really never read any of the words but I felt a longing to know what they meant. I just enjoyed flipping through the pages with the red words. I felt that there was something special about them; I just didn't know how special at the time.

Fast forward to when I had a family of my own. At the time we were living in Germany. I attended a local American church. I received my first Bible by my husband, Michael, for Mother's Day [BEST GIFT EVER]. I eventually was invited to a women's Bible study group. At the end of the class, everyone took turn to pray but when it was my turn, I didn't know what to pray. Prayer wasn't something I was familiar with. I felt embarrassed and ashamed. One of the ladies approached me and asked me if I was saved and I nervously and falsely said, "yes". I had no idea what she was talking about. Needless to say, that was my first- and last-time attending Bible Study. But on my drive home, I cried with such grief over what had happen and I couldn't figure out why. I believe a "seed" for salvation was planted that night.

Well, years past and now my family and I are back in the United States and my desire for God had really increased. So, I figured once I joined a church I would be saved. So, I joined a church (along with my family). I was baptized in water in the name of the Father, the Son and Holy Ghost after I was asked the question: Do you believe Jesus died for your sins? I said, "yes" at the time but I had a big question mark in the back of my mind of what that question meant.

After some time had passed, I was in service one day and I heard a voice ask me: "Are you sure you are saved?" At first, I just ignored it. But the question was repeated: "Are you sure you are saved?" Well, now I began to give it some thought and was wondering if I was or not and how can I be sure that I was saved. My desire to know that I was saved was growing every day. This is when Holy Spirit brought me into His Divine Classroom. He led me to the Bible my husband had given me in Germany, years ago. Now, let me pause here and share that every time I tried to read that Bible on my own, I would get a headache and I would put it away. Reading it was so hard I couldn't get through a chapter before I would be discouraged. See I believed the lie of the enemy that said I would never be able to understand the Bible. But when Holy Spirit opened my understanding, reading became more than easy, it became a delight. I developed such an appetite for the Word of God. The first book He led me to was the Gospel according to John; then the Epistles to the Romans; then the Acts of the Holy Spirit.

So, He [Holy Spirit] now takes me back to the question of salvation. He taught me how to know if I was saved or not. For one thing, I learned that salvation was not being water baptized to become a member of a church organization. These were works and salvation is not obtained by works of the flesh but through faith in Jesus Christ (Ephesians 2:8-9). Then He taught me about the fall of man, being born-again, repenting (turning away from my way thinking and the world's way and turning to God) and believing what Jesus did on the Cross (not necessarily in that order). Once Holy Spirit revealed to me that I was a sinner and separated from God, it broke my heart. I was convicted of righteous by the Holy Spirit. I remember driving home from work [my heart was so broken; my spirit was crushed] and I cried out: Jesus forgive me of my sin against You. I turned away from my way and this world's way and turn to God. I believe that You died for me on the Cross and You redeemed me back to the Father. Now I was able to believe and instantly receive eternal life. I was given the right to **become** a child of God.

Today I can confidently say "My name is written in the Lamb's Book of Life." Because I have been baptized (not water) into Jesus Christ. I have been "enveloped" into Christ.

> *Let me take a moment to teach, briefly, on baptism into Christ. To be "baptized into Christ" means that we are identified with Christ, because we have left our old or past sinful life-style and fully embrace the new life in Christ (**Mark 8:34; Luke 9:23**). When we respond to the drawing of the Holy Spirit, He "baptizes" us into the family of God in Jesus Christ (**1st Corinthians 12:13**). To be "baptized in Christ" means we have accepted His sacrifice as payment for our sin debt. And no amount of self-cleansing (water baptism) can ever make us pure enough to warrant for-giveness and a relationship with a Holy God (**Romans 3:10-12**) We can only be accepted and reconciled through the death of Jesus (**Romans 5:10**). An exchange had to take place on the Cross (**2nd Corinthians 5:21**) – His righteousness for our sinfulness. In our*

*exchange state we clothed ourselves with Christ (**Galatians 3:27**) and we have died and our life is now hidden with Christ in God (**Colossians 3:3**). Jesus suffered the punishment our sin deserves. Jesus has successfully paid in full for every act of rebellion and disobedient, past, present, and future. His work is "Finished" and His Blood is efficacious (**Hebrews 7:27**). "Baptized in Christ" means we can enter the presence of a Holy God because we are hidden in the righteousness of Christ and when God the Father looks at us, He sees His Son; He no longer sees our "filthy rags" (**Isaiah 64:6**) but He sees the righteousness of His Beloved Son (**Ephesians 2:13; Hebrews 8:12**). We are new creations in Christ (**2nd Corinthians 5:17**).*

It is in Christ we are saved. It is not by works. Walking down the church isle and shaking the pastor's hand and becoming a member of a church doesn't give a person salvation. There must be a conviction in the heart by the Holy Spirit and He must draw, and the person must believe and receive by faith the finished work of the Cross (John 1:12: Acts 20:21). Jesus is the only Mediator between God and men (1st Timothy 2:5). Christ is the Believer's hope both now and at His return. When He returns, He will deliver (1st Thessalonians 1:10; 5:4-11), He will reward (1st Thessalonians 1:19); He will perfect (1st Thessalonians 3:13), He will resurrect (1st Thessalonians 4:13-18), and He will sanctify (1st Thessalonians 5:23) all who put their trust in Him.

So, there are three major works performed by the Holy Spirit in preparing the unsaved to become a child of God:

Restraining – Satan is seeking who he can devour (1st Peter 5:8) and would enjoy nothing more than to destroy (John 10:10) people before they make their decision to accept Christ as Savior and Lord. But the

Holy Spirit works to prevent this from occurring (but not against a person's will) (Isaiah 59:19).

Convicting – Holy Spirit works in convicting mankind of sin and righteousness. We can see this in Acts when Apostle Peter addressed the crowd on the day of Pentecost. When the crowd heard him, many were convicted in their hearts to put faith in Jesus Christ. "Now when they heard this, they were pricked in their heart, and said unto Peter and to the rest of the apostles, Men and brethren, what shall we do? (2:37).

Regeneration – When a repenting sinner accepts Christ as Savior, the Holy Spirit gives him a new nature (2nd Corinthians 5:17). Jesus told Nicodemus about being born-again by the Holy Spirit (John 3:3-7).

Requirements of Salvation:

Confession – Acts 2:21

Repentance – Mark 1:15

Faith – John 3:14-18 – It is not faith **in what is heard** but faith that comes **by what is heard [the message of Jesus Christ]**

Regeneration – John 3:3-8

Holy Scripture – 2 Timothy 3:15

Salvation is available to all who put faith in Jesus and Him alone (John 14:6; Acts 4:12) and is dependent on God alone for provision, assurance, and security. A mighty man of God said, "At what age you die does not matter. The nature of death does not matter. What matters is where you are going." –Prophet T. B. Joshua (SCOAN).

Make sure you **Do Not** leave this life without Salvation. *"The grace of our Lord Jesus Christ be with you all, Amen." Revelation 22:21*

Thirteen

༄

The Holy Spirit and the Cross

"Christ, who through the eternal Spirit offered Himself without blemish to God."
Hebrews 9:14 ERV

It was this Spirit that was in Christ from the womb, that taught His to concerning the obedience of the Cross as stated in Luke 2:49 about being about His Father's business. It was the Holy Spirit that led Jesus in baptism to humble Himself to be treated as a sinner and to prepare Him for the death on the Cross. It was this Spirit that led Him into the wilderness. It was through this Spirit, that He was led step by step to speak of, meet, and bear all He had to suffer. It is the Holy Spirit of God dwelling in flesh that leads inevitably and triumphantly to the Cross.

Jesus didn't just die to take our sin away, but He took the punishment we deserved. He took the judgement on Himself and God's wrath. His death on the Cross justified us not His resurrection. His resurrection gives us new life and the power to live the new life by the power of the Holy Ghost. The power for this new life is not supernatural but it is divine Holy power.

The life of a Christian begins at the Cross and a true believer must trust in the Cross. Why? Because the Believer's life and the Cross are inseparable. the Cross is not measured by time. The Lamb has been slain from the foundation of the world (Revelation 13:8).

The Holy Spirit and Christ's work on Calvary's Cross is a wonderful partnership. We know that Jesus gave His life on the Cross, and it is the Holy Spirit who makes the Cross effectual in the believer through salvation (1st Corinthians 12:3). The Holy Spirit makes the Cross more that an annual event, but He makes it an operation. He continues to reveal and illuminate the fuller meaning of Christ's Cross.

We must understand that the Cross of Christ is not to make us better but to condemn and put to death the flesh. But just as equally, the flesh desires to cast aside and conquer the Cross. We must understand that our entire old nature is sentenced to death and must become dead by the Cross, so that the new life in Christ may come to rule in us. It is the Holy Spirit that gives us insight into the fallen condition of our old nature and its enmity against God. Therefore, we must become willing and desirous to be wholly freed from it (the old nature). Romans 7:18 teaches that in our flesh dwells nothing good. The carnal mind is enmity against God, and it cannot be subject to God's law (Romans 8:7). When we believe God's word (Galatians 5:24) and long to be delivered from the old nature and learn to love the Cross as our deliverer from the power of the enemy, the Holy Spirit will work mightily in our new life. For it is at the Cross a spiritual heart circumcision takes place. "In Him you were also circumcised with a circumcision made without hands, in the removal of the sinful nature by the Circumcision of Christ (Colossians 2:11-13). The sacrifice of Jesus's death on the Cross brought us a divine exchange from God for our wicked heart for the heart of Christ.

So, what is this divine exchange we inherited? Remember in Ezekiel 36:26-27 it stated that the exchange of the New Covenant God would replace our old sin-hardened heart with His new spiritual heart. Galatians 2:20 gives biblical evidence of the foundation of this exchange: *I have been crucified with Christ and I no longer live, but Christ lives in me. The life I now live in the body, I live by faith in the Son of God, who loved me and gave himself for me.* "God made Christ who had no sin to be sin for us, so that we might become the righteousness of God in Him (2nd Corinthians

5:21). In other words, Christ exchanged our unholy nature with His holy nature and reconciled us to God (Romans 5:10; 1ˢᵗ Corinthians 1:30; Colossians 1:21-22; 1ˢᵗ Peter 2:24; 1ˢᵗ John 5:11-12). By the sacrifice of Christ Jesus, God translated us from Adam's sinful nature into Christ's divine nature (2ⁿᵈ Peter 1:4). When we are born-again by the Spirit (John 3:3-8), our sinful nature is crucified and removed (Romans 6:6; Colossians 2:11) and we become a new creation in Christ (2ⁿᵈ Corinthians 5:17; Galatians 1:16; 2:20; and Colossians 1:27). Thus, the Christian life is not a "changed life" it is an "exchanged life". Our old nature was beyond repair, and it could not be made better. God's aim was to totally dispose of the old nature and exchange it for Christ's nature. The old mind set sinfulness, rebellion, disobedience and self-righteousness would not reconcile or redeem the sinner back to God.

In the divine exchange, our new life is now hidden with Christ in God (Colossians 3:3). This is the divine operation of the Cross that Holy Spirit provides. Thus, the divine operation and exchange was spiritual not physical. It occurs in our spirit not our body. This is a miraculous inward transformation has taken place in our spirit but who we are in Christ is not yet fully visible. We receive the continued sanctification by the Holy Spirit. "When Christ, who is our live, is revealed, then you will be revealed with Him in glory (Colossians 3:4). This a part of the eternal redemption which Jesus Christ has wrought for us. On our own, we cannot grasp with our understanding or accomplish with our strength. It comes from abiding in the Lord Jesus, day by day. It is something in which the Holy Spirit will teach us, and He will impart it to us an experience, and will show how He gives victory in the power of the Cross over all that is of the flesh. God has given us two great powers from heaven, namely, the Cross and the [Holy] Spirit. It is through the constant and consistent abiding fellowship of the Cross. Most rely on what the Cross has purchased for them, on forgiveness of sin and peace with God, but they can go a lifetime without fellowship with the Lord Himself. Why is this? I believe that the hindrance lies in the fact that the Church is too much under the sway of the flesh and the world. There is not enough teaching and understanding of the heart piercing power of the Cross of

Christ. Many in the congregations complain that the subject is too high or too deep. But the Holy Spirit is waiting and willing to take all who desire under His teaching and to make known the secret of the spiritual life above all expectations. He is prepared to take them under teaching to lead them to the Cross, and His divine operation. The Holy Spirit wants to reveal the neglect of the inner being.

There is always the battle between the flesh and the Spirit (Galatians 5:16-17). Although the flesh has been defeated at the Cross, it will still attempt to do as much damage to us as possible against the stronger force of the Spirit. Even after a person has been raised to life by the Holy Spirit, the old sinful desires of the flesh do not willing go away. There is still a battle that rages on. Therefore, we must understand that our entire nature is sentenced to death and must become dead by the Cross, so that the new life in Christ may come to take dominion in us and over us as Lord. Again, I say, there must be revelation of the fallen condition of our nature and its enmity against God. God wants us to know the eternal value and power of the Cross. He wants us to know that the newness of Cross results in power, love, victory and patience. The newness of the Cross remains unchanged throughout time. If were intentional concerning the reality of the death of Jesus is new before us, our having been crucified with Him shall also remain unchanged in our life. "Then Jesus said to His disciples, "If anyone wants to come after Me, let him deny himself, and take up his cross and be following Me. For whoever wants to save his life will lose it. But whoever loses his life for My sake will find it. For what will a person be profited if he gains the whole world, but forfeits his life? Or what will a person give in-exchange-for his life? (Matthew 16:24-26). The Holy Spirit empowers us to carry this out through the power of Cross of Christ.

Here's the thing, if we are ignorant or don't believe that on the Cross, we died with Christ (2nd Timothy 2:11; Colossians 2:20; Galatians 2:20; Romans 6:6), we will not be delivered. If we do not listen to His Word and allow the Holy Spirit to work in us but instead choose to look upon our situation, we will never enter into the reality of our flesh have been crucified. What matters is that God has pronounced our flesh crucified and therefore it is crucified. Regardless of our feelings and experience, we have to respond to God's Word with faith to experience our flesh crucified on the Cross by the power of the Holy Spirit. It is God's purpose and plan to crucify the old man with Christ so that our spirit, soul, and body can be restored to their original position as created by God in the beginning. It is our responsibility to acknowledge and agree with God's Word and believe it by faith. In this our faith in what Christ has already accomplished allows the Holy Spirit to make this real in our life. Thus, based on the faith we have in His Word, the Holy Spirit realigns our living condition (what we experience of God's complete work) with our legal position (what God has done for us). It is stated in Colossians 3:3, "You have died." This is our legal position and in Colossians 3:5 it is stated, "Therefore put to death." This is our living condition. The victory that Cross gives comes first by identifying with His death. And we rely on the Holy Spirit to work in us to put our flesh to death (Romans 8:13). When we put knowing, believing, and depending upon the [Holy] Spirit's power, they all work together to make this death experience real in life. But be mindful that this spiritual death is not a once for all proposition, but it is daily. Whenever we aren't watchful and prayerful, the flesh will certainly go on a rampage. As a new creation, we need to be renewed day by day (2nd Corinthians 4:16) and empowered with the power of the Holy Spirit. I like to say, it is daily, hour by hour even moment by moment I need to be in the gradual and perpetual process of being renewed. This renewal is a process that goes on throughout our Christian life (Romans 6:4; 7:6). Our renewal is by the Cross, the Holy Spirit and the Word of God.

As Children of God, we must seek for a higher life and service for His glory and the advancement of His Kingdom. We are at the terminal period of the dispensation of grace. The hour is at hand and the Church has to turn away from apostasy and turn back to God. The world is becoming more gloomier and darken day by day. The Cross of Christ is the sole light that enlightens this darkness. It is time to get back to the foundation of faith and it starts as the Cross of Christ. It is at the Cross and by the power of the Holy Spirit that are sins are remitted (to dismiss;

set free), we were cleansed, given power over sin and delivered. It is at the Cross and by the Spirit that the redemptive facts of God are revealed for us to believe and enter in. It is time to return to the Cross not as an even but as an operation. To be born again is to be crucified at the Cross of Christ in the power of the Holy Spirit. I pray for the Church of God be re-awakened to her calling as the light in the world and salt of the earth. I pray that she will stand in the victory of Christ and bring back the King of kings and Lord of lords.

It is through the Cross of Christ and the by the power of the Holy Spirit we are made flawless and blameless, even in this present age. We must remember what was exchanged on the Cross. First remember, Christ was exchanged for us. We can say that we are "Barabbas" that was released, and Jesus was crucified. Just like Jesus took "Barabbas" place on the Cross, He took our place also. Here are some Scriptures to give evidence of the divine exchange.

Jesus was punished that we might be forgiven. (Isaiah 53:6, 10; Romans 5:1)

Jesus was wounded that we might be healed. (Isaiah 53:4; 1st Peter 2:24)

Jesus was made sin with our sinfulness that we might be made righteous with His righteousness. (2nd Corinthians 5:21; Isaiah 53:10)

Jesus was made died our death that we might receive His life. (Romans 6:23)

Jesus endured our poverty that we might share His abundance. (2nd Corinthians 8:9; 9:8).

Jesus bore our shame that we might share His glory. (John 17: 22; Hebrews 12:2)

Jesus endured our rejection that we might have His acceptance with the Father. (Matthew 27:46, 50; Ephesians 1:5-6)

Jesus was made a curse that we might enter into the blessing. (Galatians 3:13; Deuteronomy 21:23)

When we put on Christ (Romans 13:14) by the power of the Holy Spirit, we can declare that the Cross of Christ is ENOUGH!

1. Jesus has taken my rebellion and independence and I have restored daily fellowship with God.
2. Jesus removed my darkened heart and I have received a new heart, alight with God's desires.
3. Jesus removed my sinfulness and now I daily put on Christ's robe of righteousness.
4. Jesus removed the power of sin and now I have the power and passion to live in holiness.
5. Jesus has taken my shame and now I radiate His glory.
6. Jesus removed the curse. I walk by the Spirit, experiencing God's blessings.
7. Jesus has taken my sickness and I live in divine health.

Through the Cross and the [Holy] Spirit Jesus removed my rebellion, my evil heart desires, my overt sins, my enslavement to sin, my shame, my curse, my sickness, my poverty, my sorrow, my anxiety, my fear of rejection, and my death. Therefore, I confess I am complete in Christ (Colossians 1:28). Jesus has given me restored fellowship, new heart desires, His righteousness, power over sin, His glory, the Holy Spirit, health, prosperity, hope, joy, peace, adoption into His family and eternal life.

The Spirit alone reveals the meaning of the Cross and teach its fellowship. It is the [Holy] Spirit who led Jesus to the Cross; the Cross leads us to Jesus and the outpouring of the Spirit; then the Spirit leads us back to the Cross. We must put our confidence in the finished work of the Cross. We are to live as crucified with Christ. Thus, we are to walk as Believers who have crucified the flesh and the only way to conquer it is by every hour regarding it as crucified (Galatians 2:20; 5:24; 6:14). I believe that the most perfect expression of the mind of the Holy Spirit is the Cross. It is God who takes possession of the human nature to free it from sin and fill it with Himself through crucifying it. So, what God demands, the Holy Spirit works. The Holy Spirit brings us into fellowship with the Cross.

For those who are enemies of the Cross of Christ, their destiny is destruction, their god is their stomach, and their glory is in their shame. Their mind is on earthly things. They pursue worldly things and possessions that will one day pass away (Philippians 3:18-19). Although they profess the name of Christ they actually do not belong to Christ (Matthew 7:15; 21).

"But our citizenship is in heaven. And we eagerly await a Savior from there, the Lord Jesus Christ, who, by the power that enables him to bring everything under his control, will transform our lowly bodies so that they will be like his glorious body." Philippians 3:20-21

Fourteen

~

Acts of the Holy Spirit

"But ye, shall receive power, after that the Holy Ghost is come upon you: and ye shall be witnesses unto me both in Jerusalem, and in all Judea, and in Samaria, and unto the uttermost part of the earth." Acts 1:8

The Book of Acts is not just a historical book of the early Church, but it is a book for the new life and for a Spirit-filled Church. Because of Luke's strong emphasis on the ministry of the Holy Spirit, some refer to it as the Acts of the Spirit of Christ working through and in the apostles. There should be a desire and expectation for Believers for elements in the New Testament Church's ministry and experience to be a norm for today's Church. The same thing is attainable when the Church moves in the full power of the Holy Spirit. Now I know there are some in the Church who things that signs, wonders, miracles, spiritual gifts, or the apostolic standard for the Church's life and ministry ceased at the end of the apostolic age. However, I am with those who believe that they do still happen, and the apostolic age has not ended. They are given both for the blessing of the Church and for the spread of the gospel. Acts records what the Church must be and do in any generation as it continues Jesus' ministry in the power of the Holy Spirit. It must be remembered that sign, miracles, and wonders weren't given just to the first century apostles. [Because remember Stephen and Philip weren't apostles but did, they great wonders and miraculous signs among the people (Acts 6:8; Acts 8:5-6)]. Just as God had a pattern for the tabernacle under the Old Covenant, God has a pattern for His Church under the New Covenant. It wasn't the apostles who decided how the Church was to be structured. It was God the Father and God the Son, through and by the power of the Holy Spirit who established the apostolic pattern for the Church. The tragic thing is that after the first century Church, there has been a gradual departure from divine revelation and modification of God's heavenly pattern by accommodating and compromising both culturally and organizationally according to human ideas and human wisdom.

In order for the Church of Christ to experience the full plan, power, and presence of God again, she must turn from her own ways and embrace the New Testament apostolic pattern as God's divine standard for the Church. The Church has to refuse to disobey God and His Word, turn her heart back to the ways and lifestyle of the godly, and stop resisting the Holy Spirit. Jesus said in John 14:12, "Truly, truly, I tell you, whoever believes in Me will also do the works that I am doing. He will do greater things than these, because I am going to the Father." I believe the Word of the Lord. In other words, Jesus is the same yesterday, today and forever and the Holy Spirit is still present and active among the people of God. Of course, faith plays a major role. The faith that is a faith in Jesus Christ to do what He has promised and a faith in the Holy Spirit to be everything Jesus said He would be for a life full of the Holy Spirit. Every born-again believer should desire for something more than nominal Christianity, nominal Church services, and nominal ministry efforts but we should so hunger and thirst for our hearts to be stirred until it transforms from a flickering flame to a raging fire. Jesus, Himself, declared, "Blessed are those who hunger and thirst for righteousness, for they shall be filled." (Matthew 5:6). The Holy Spirit is essential for the advancement and expansion of the Kingdom of God. The baptism of the Holy Spirit is not for a one-generation event. We need to receive the divine power of the Holy Spirit in our lives and our ministries in order to serve God successfully in the earth.

Holy Spirit is not a natural person with supernatural powers. He is a Divine Person just like God the Father. God gives the Holy Spirit to work miracles among us by the divine power of God (Galatians 3:5) not by supernatural power. We read in John 3:5 those born from water and the Spirit are born not of natural descent, nor human decision or a husband's will, but born of God (John 1:12-13). Take note that is not of natural descent, which is why supernatural is not the correct representation of the power of the Holy Spirit. Those born of God are spirit because God is Spirit. We are born from above. We are spiritual being becoming like Christ. And we have to stop thinking as human-doings and start thinking as spirit-beings born of God. Our DNA (Divine Nature Accepted) is totally different, and we take on a new nature not natural but divine. Therefore, we have to stop referring to God His power as supernatural. God is not natural – He is Spirit, and we are to put off the old nature and put on the new nature of Christ. Thus, we are called Christians (without **Christ – I – am – nothing**).

Through the anointing of Holy Spirit, we receive divine spiritual power for this newborn-again life. God does not give us supernatural powers – There is nowhere in the Bible that refers to believers being given supernatural powers. God is not trying to give us power to operate in our natural. Flesh and blood can't inherit the Kingdom of God. The Spirit gives life and the flesh counts for nothing. Remember those controlled by the [sinful] nature cannot please God (Romans 8:8).

The work of bringing the Good News to the ends of the earth is far from finished. As the people of God, we are called to continue the effort by the power of the Holy Spirit.

Listed are the occurrences of the Holy Spirit in Acts.

Chapter 1:2,5,16

Chapter 2:3,4,33,38,43

Chapter 3:8,25,31,33

Chapter 4:8,25,31,33

Chapter 5:3,9,32 (The Holy Spirit is given to those who obey God)
Chapter 6:3,5,8,10
Chapter 7:51,55
Chapter 8:15,16,17,18,19,20,29,39
Chapter 9:17,51 (The Church was strengthened and encouraged by Holy Spirit)
Chapter 10:19,38,44,45,47 (the pouring out of the Spirit brings tongues)
Chapter 11:12,15,16,24,28
Chapter 12:7,23
Chapter 13:2,4,9,52
Chapter 14:3,27
Chapter 15:8,28
Chapter 16:6,7
Chapter 17:
Chapter 18:9
Chapter 19:2,6,11
Chapter 20:22,23,26
Chapter 21:4,11
Chapter 22:7,8,10
Chapter 23:11
Chapter 28:25

Miracles by the Holy Spirit

- The Believers in the Upper were baptized and filled by the Holy Spirit and spoke in other tongues – Acts 2:1-4
- Everyone is awestruck by the miracles done through the apostles – Acts 2:43
- Peter heals a man lame from birth – Acts 3:2-10; 4:16, 22
- The apostles perform many signs and wonders, healings and exorcisms; Peter's mere shadow has healing power – Acts 5:12-16
- An angel rescues the apostles from prison – Acts 5:18-20
- Stephen performs signs and wonders – Acts 6:8

- Philip performs signs, healings and exorcisms in Samaria – Acts 8:6-7
- Philip's signs and miracles amaze Simon the Sorcerer – Acts 8:13
- The spirit of the Lord snatches Philip from the road to Gaza and places him in Azotus – Acts 8:39-40
- Saul's conversion, blindness and healing at the hands of Ananias – Acts 9:1-18; 22:6-13; 26:12-18
- Peter heals Aeneas in Lydd - Acts 9:33-34
- Peter raises Tabitha/Dorcas – Acts 9:36-41
- An angel rescues Peter from prison – Acts 12:6-11
- Paul strikes Bar-Jesus/Elymas blind – Acts 13:6-11
- Paul and Barnabas perform signs and wonders in Phrygian Iconium – Acts 14:3
- Paul heals a man lame from birth – Acts 14:8-10
- Paul and Barnabas recount the signs and wonders performed among non-Jews – Acts 15:12
- Paul casts out a spirit of divination – Acts 16:16-18
- An earthquake happened as Paul and Silas prayed and sang in prison – Acts 16:26
- God works "unusual miracles" through Paul: garments that have merely touched him have healing power – Acts 19:11-12
- Paul raises Eutychus after he falls from a third-floor window – Acts 20:9-10
- Paul survives a viper's bite- Acts 28:3-6
- Paul heals the father of Publius and others - Acts 28:8-9

Fifteen

~~

The Holy Spirit -the Power of the Church

"And I say to you that you are Peter, and on this rock I will build My Church; and the gates of Hades (death) will not overpower it [by preventing the resurrection of the Christ]." **Matthew 16:18 AMP**

"The is not merely a meeting; the Church is not for a kind of activity; the Church is not for a kind of service or for anything else. The Church is absolutely to express Christ." Witness Lee

After Peter's confession that Jesus was the Christ, the Son of the living God (Matthew 16:16), which was revealed by God the Father, Jesus made the above declaration about victory for the Church. He said that the gates of hell will not prevail against the Church. In other words, nothing will be able to stand against the Church. Jesus promises Peter and the other apostles that He would give them the keys of the Kingdom of Heaven. Just from using keys in our everyday life, we know that keys are for locking and unlocking doors. I believe the keys Jesus spoke about are concerning revelations from Heaven such as Peter received. Here Jesus is laying the foundation of His Church (Ephesians 2:20). Peter and the other disciples would be the apostolic blueprint to enter into the kingdom. In other words, Jesus was giving them the authority to allow and disallow according to heaven and invite the world to enter. Remember Jesus told Nicodemus that unless one is born again, they will not see the Kingdom of Heaven (John 3:3). And we know that we can only be born again from above by the Spirit of God. It would be by the Holy Spirit that Peter stood up and preached on the Day of Pentecost. It was by filling of the Holy Spirit that Peter preached to everyone there by one language and I believe the Holy Ghost allowed them to hear in each of their languages.

But even before the outpouring of the Holy Spirit upon the disciples in the upper room, John's account of the gospel events has Jesus breathing on them to receive the Holy Spirit (John 20:22). Jesus is not the same as the baptism of the Spirit in the upper room. Now I believe at this moment the disciples became born again of the Spirit. I believe it was the disciples' initial new covenant experience of the regenerating presence of the Holy Spirit and the impartation of new life from the resurrected Christ. They were made new creations in Christ. This event fulfilled what Jesus told them in John 14:17, But you know him (Holy Spirit), for he (Holy Spirit) lives with you and will be in you." This was completed after Jesus was resurrected and glorified when He breathed on them and said to them receive the Holy Spirit.

In my research by the leading of Holy Spirit, the word in the Greek for "breathed" is emphusao'. This is the same verb used in the Septuagint (The Greek translation of the OT) at Genesis 2:7, where God breathed in Adam's nostrils the breath of life and he became a living being. So, when John uses this word, it explains to us that Jesus was giving the Spirit in order to bring forth life and a new creation. When Jesus breathed on them, they were now born from above; born of the Spirit. Now because of His resurrection Jesus became the life-giving spirit (1st Corinthians 15:45). This was a historical moment for the Church. Because at that moment Jesus said, "receive the Holy Spirit", He began to live in the disciples. In the Greek, the word used for "receive" means a single act of reception. The Holy Spirit was given to regenerate them, to make them new creatures in Christ (2ⁿᵈCorinthians 5:17).

It is true that the disciples were true believers and followers of Jesus, but they were saved according to the old covenant provisions. Therefore, they were not yet regenerated in the new covenant sense. Up until this point in John 20:22, they had not entered the new covenant provisions based on the death, burial and resurrection of Jesus (Matthew 26:28; Luke 22:20; 1ˢᵗ Corinthians 11:25; Ephesians 2:15-16; Hebrews 9:15-17). In John 3:1-8, Jesus teaches on the foundational doctrine of the Christian faith: spiritual birth or regeneration. Without the new birth one cannot see the Kingdom of God. Without the new birth, no one can receive eternal life and salvation through Jesus Christ. Remember prior to turning to Christ by faith, humans in their inherent nature are sinners who are spiritually dead and are incapable of obeying and pleasing God (Psalm 51:5; Jeremiah 17:9; Romans 8:7-8; 1ˢᵗ Corinthians 2:14; Ephesians 2:3). Therefore, a re-creating of spiritual life in the human heart is needed (Romans 12:2; Ephesians 4:23-24) by the Holy Spirit (John 3:6; Titus 3:5). It is at this time the Church was technically born not on the day of Pentecost. The spiritual birth of the disciples at this time and the birth of the Church are one and the same. See the language in Acts 2:41 when it states that "and that same day there were added unto them about 3,000 souls. In other words, the 3,000 believers were added to those who were already born again.

We must get the understanding of John 20:22 and Acts 2:4. It is crucial in understanding the ministry of the Holy Spirit to God's people. We are given two true statements from these verses: the disciples were breathed on and received the Holy Spirit; they were indwelt and regenerated by the Holy Spirit before the Day of Pentecost and the outpouring of the Spirit in Acts 2:4 was an experience occurring after their regeneration by the Holy Spirit. What took place in John 20:22 was the first work of the Holy Spirit in the birthing of the Church and the baptism of the Holy Spirit in Acts 2:4 was a second distinct work of the Spirit in them. This sets the foundation of the Church and is normative for all Christians.

In other words, all believers receive the Holy Spirit at the time of their regeneration or rebirth and either at that point or at another time must experience (at least they should) the baptism in the Spirit for empowering them to be His witness (Acts 1:5, 8; 2:4). We must not be deceived into believing that the baptism of the Holy Spirit was only for those in the upper room. On the contrary, the promise of the baptism of the Holy Spirit is for all who would believe in Christ. Acts 2:39 states, "The promise is for you and your children and for all who are far off, for all whom the Lord our God will call." Today's believers are included in this passage. I submit to you that the baptism in the Spirit of God and power was not a once-for-all occurrence in the Church history. No, this did not stop with Pentecost. I submit that the baptism of the Spirit is the birth-right of every faith believer in Jesus Christ to seek, expect and experience today. Christ is united in us through the Holy Spirit because Christ is the Spirit, and the Spirit is the very reality of Christ (1st Corinthians 15:45b; 2nd Corinthians 3:17). If we have the Holy Spirit, we have Christ.

It is of utmost importance that believers recognize the importance of Holy Spirit in God's redemptive purpose. In the Church, the Holy Spirit is the agent of service that empowers believers for service and witness. Jesus commanded the disciples to wait for the promise of the Father because they would be baptized with the Holy Spirit for power to be wit-nesses (Acts 1:4-8). When believers are baptized in the Spirit, we receive power to witness for Christ and work effectively within the Church and before the world. This is the same Spirit that descended on Jesus at the time of His baptism by John in the Jordan River (John 1:32-33). It is the same Spirit that raised Jesus from the dead. Yes, and it is God's intended purpose that all disciples of Christ experience the baptism in the Holy Spirit. The baptism of the Spirit is different from the filling of the Spirit (I will discuss this in another chapter).

The lack of teaching has led to not understanding the role or ministry of the Holy Spirit in the Church. Why is this so important? Because Holy Spirit is the power of God in the Church. The Church is a spiritual ministry and cannot function or be a channel for God without the Spirit. Holy Spirit is given as a gift for the Church. He brings Believers into union with Christ and equips them with spiritual gifts that is used to serve the Church. Holy Spirit gives the Church the ability to say "no" to the sinful nature and to overcome the power of sin. It is Holy Spirit who bears witness with the Believer's spirit that they belong to Christ (Romans 8:16). The Holy Spirit is the Lord in the Church and to neglect His leading will lead to spiritual neglect and spiritual complacency. Could it be that many in the Body of Christ does not recognize the Holy Spirit as a person? For the most part, the Church knows and claims a very small part of that which God has made possible in Christ, because she knows so little of what the Holy Spirit can do for her and longs to do for her.

The Church is the called-out ones. In the Greek, it refers to an assembly of people summoned together. The Church is the congregation of God's people in Christ and Christ is the Head. Because the Church is the Body of Christ, she cannot function the way God intends for her to function without Holy Spirit. Holy Spirit is the power of God working in us and building His Church through Believers. Therefore, it is essential to understand that nothing works without Holy Spirit. The Church is ineffective without Holy Spirit. There is no life without Him. Many congregations operate without the power of the Spirit of God. Instead, people become more dependent upon human wisdom, rituals, routines, and traditions. The Church is so structured, and I believe it leaves no room for Holy Spirit to usher in the presence of true worship. Think about it – we come to church, sing about three songs, pray, hear announcements, take a couple of offerings, listen to a sermon, then an invitation to join the church; maybe another prayer and benediction. I am not knocking any of these, but do we really want Holy Spirit to be in control of the service so that the manifest presence of God will show up. The real manifest presence of God is when He shows up and shows out. He comes to take over and the program outline is no longer followed. Emotionalism will turn into true worship in spirit and in truth. In the Old Testament, 2nd Chronicles 5:14 tells us that when the glory of God filled the house of God, the priest couldn't even stand to minister. The people fell on the face in reverent worship. I believe some of our churches today can use that kind of shaking up. The Holy Spirit would shake out sin, apathy, pride, self-centeredness, and satisfaction with Church as unusual and humanism. We don't need more programs and fundraisers; we need the presence and power of a Holy God.

Now this is my opinion, but I am convinced that before this pandemic Church attendance was on a decrease in attendance. One of the reasons for this, I believe, is that the church looks too much like the world. There seems to be no difference, no distinction. There is no love or unity within the same church. In essence, the church has become explainable and compromising. Some churches are so well-oiled, they desire to be efficient and cater to the flesh and to satisfy itchy ears. The focus seems to be on the people rather than on the presence of God. Church programs and other activities does not change a person's life for eternity. They don't lead to maturity. You can say: come as you are and leave as you came. Without the Holy Spirit working in the Church, too many people walk out the same way they came. Jesus said that He is the way, the truth, and the life. We need to allow Holy Spirit to do what He is sent to do. If the Church is not careful, she will forget her purpose (Matthew 28:18-20; Mark 16:15). Services will turn into attracting people rather than attracting the presence of God and seeking His face. He will then attract the people. If we draw near to God, He will draw near to us (James 4:8). He is the true audience. We should not seek numbers but seek Jesus! He will do the adding just like He did with the first century Church in the book of Acts. We must seek His Kingdom and His righteous above all else (Matthew 6:33). The Spirit is speaking. We must make it a priority and desire to hear what He is saying to the Church.

> [3] Howbeit when he, the Spirit of truth, is come, he will guide you into all truth: for he shall not speak of himself; but whatsoever he shall hear, that shall he speak: and he will shew you things to come.
>
> [14] He shall glorify me: for he shall receive of mine, and shall shew it unto you.
>
> [15] All things that the Father hath are mine: therefore said I, that he shall take of mine, and shall shew it unto you. (John 16:13-15)

Singing praise songs, shouting, dancing, running around the Church is all well and good, but that is not the priority or the purpose of the Church. It is not the mandate that was given by Jesus Christ. So, believe that being loud and noisy in service is something to brag about but remember the Church at Sardis in the Book of Revelation? In 3:1-2, Jesus said plainly, "You have a name that you are alive, but you are dead. Wake up and strengthen the things that remain, which were about to die; for I have not found your deed completed in the sight of My God."

Here is the thing, God's work is intended to be done by His Power, which is the Holy Spirit. There was a work for the Church to do and Jesus promised that the Father would send the Holy Spirit after He has ascended back to the Father. Jesus told the disciples to tarry in Jerusalem until they Holy Spirit gave them power to carry out the mandate. In Acts 1:4-5 states, "And, being assembled with them, commanded them that they should not depart from Jerusalem, but wait for the promise of the Father, which, saith He, ye have heard of Me. For John truly baptized with water; but ye shall be baptized with the Holy Ghost not many days hence."

The Holy Spirit is the One who birth the early Church. He is the keeper and sustainer of the Church today. He is the Lord in the Church and the power of the Church. The Church really needs to allow the Holy Spirit to lead and guide every aspect of God's House. He knows exactly and specifically what to do and how to do it and who to do it through. Glory to God! I am getting excited right about now!!! Like the first century disciples, we need to obey the command and wait for the Holy Spirit to show up (Acts 2:1-4). I believe that there needs to be an emphasis on Holy Spirit in the Church. I love Holy Spirit. In the effort of some churches to become "relevant" and promote membership increase, the Holy Spirit and His ministry has been neglected. Some leaders even limit the move of the Holy Spirit because of compromise. Yet churches that welcome Holy Spirit and allow Him to lead are criticized for not following their way. Listen, I choose being anointed with the Holy Spirit then using human wisdom, talent, and charisma. I don't need the latest fashion, catchy sermon titles, motivational messages, or catch phrases.

But just give me the Holy Spirit and nothing else and I will have everything. Know this when the Church leaves out the Holy Spirit, she begins to use systems and human strategies. Yet there is no substitute for the Divine Power and Presence of Holy Spirit because methods of men cannot take the place of His power. Organized programs cannot substitute His power. Systematic structure cannot substitute His Spirit. Why would the Church want to settle for less than the Holy Spirit? The Church can no longer minimize the Holy Spirit because when they minimize the role of the Holy Spirit, they minimize Christ.

God has called the Church, the Body of Christ, to live by the power of the Holy Spirit. He is needed for the Church to show what a godly community look like, and the early Church has left an example for Believers today. Acts 2:42-47 records this of the early Church:

> "They were continually devoting themselves to the apostle's teaching and to fellowship, to the breaking of bread and to prayer. Everyone kept feeling a sense of awe; and many wonders and signs were taking place through the apostles. And all those who had believed were together and had all things in common; and they began selling their property and possessions and were sharing them will all, as anyone might have need. Day by day continuing with one mind in the temple, and breaking bread from house to house, they were taking their meals together with gladness and sincerity of heart, praising God and having favor with all the people. And the Lord was adding to their number day by day those who were being saved."

This is the true community. The first century Church really experienced the kind of love that Jesus taught His disciples in John 13:35. Love is the true mark of an authentic Follower of Christ. When the Church today lives as the Church in Acts, I can only imagine the glory that would be given to God.

The early Church was devoted to study and learn God's Word. It was a priority for them to take in as much teaching about God's Word as possible. Time wasn't an issue. Unlike some congregations today, if the message goes over 30 minutes, people are angry. It has even been said that the people's attention span is not that long. Eternity has no end. I believe it is time for the real Church of God in Christ Jesus to get back to the basics and foundation of the Church. It is time that the Church start looking like Christ, talking, and walking like Christ. There must be such a hunger and thirst for the Word of God like never before, especially in these end times. We should have such an appetite for the Word of God that it is always in our thoughts and on our lips. It should be that nothing else can satisfy our spiritual appetite but the Word of God. The bible teaches that man shall not live by bread alone but by every word that comes from the mouth of God. We must develop such an appetite for the Word of God in which we approach it as if it was our very life, food, and sustenance. As spiritual humans, we need the Word of God each day. Apostle Paul wrote in 2nd Timothy 3:16 "All scripture is given by inspiration of God, and is profitable for doctrine, for reproof, for correction, for instruction in righteousness" – the Word of God is given so that every woman and man of God may be perfect, thoroughly equipped to do good works (vs. 17). In other words, the Bible gives principles to the new creation to live by and we must obey it. When we read, teach, and preach the Bible, we believe it is God's Truth.

It is Holy Spirit who brings the Church in a relationship with Christ. It is through the Unity of the Spirit that Believers are united as the Body of Christ with Christ as the head. And we know that the ultimate purpose of the Church is to bring honor and glory to its head. By the power of Holy Spirit, the Church fulfills this purpose as it related to God's program for the world. John 3:16 states that God loved the world so much that He sent His only begotten Son in the world to be saved. This program is specifically spelled out in the Great Commission as written in Matthew 28:19-20. The Great Commission has not been recalled by God, but the disciples of Christ are to "teach all nations" by baptizing them in the name of the Father, and of the Son, and of the Holy Ghost and by "teaching them to observe all things whatsoever He has commanded us. Teaching is absolutely necessary for spiritual transformation and spiritual growth. As Believers, we are commanded to grow in the knowledge of God through Jesus Christ. In Ephesians chapter four, the Holy Spirit enables Christians to learn their spiritual walk rooted in their spiritual wealth. In other words, Ephesians focuses on the believer's responsibility to walk accordance with their heavenly calling in Christ Jesus (4:1). It encourages the Body of Christ as a whole to mature in Christ. Therefore, the Church must be aware of her position in Christ because this is the basis of her practice in this life. Christ has set up roles in the Church to function for the support and maturity of His people (Ephesians 4). Verse 11 states, And he gave some, apostles; and some, prophets; and some, evangelists; and some, pastors and teachers. The key to understanding Ephesians 4:11 can be found in a study of the Greek words Paul used and comparing them with what he said about their purpose in verses 12 and 13. The word for apostle means ambassador or commissioner, the one for prophet means foreteller, evangelist means preacher, pastor means shepherd, and teacher means instructor. Their combined purpose is to bring unity, maturity, and purity to the body of Christ. (I think the position of pastor became the senior one among these when we began paying pastors as professionals and giving them ultimate authority over local congregations. But as Ephesians 4:11-12 indicates, this was not the original intention.)

Consequently, the only way the Church can walk worthy of the vocation she was called is by the power and presence of the Holy Spirit. The Church cannot just say they are the Church without evidence of a transformation but there must be evidence of this transformation. Just like it would be a pitiful sight to see an adult head on an infant's body, likewise, the body of Christ and Christ as the head but His body is still an infant. The Believers must come to the place where they realize that the new life gives them a new position in Christ and that position must have the practice along with it. This practice must include the unity of all Believers in the body of Christ to grow and mature coming to the effectual working of every member by the power of the Holy Spirit (Ephesians 4:16).

If the Church does not reclaim the Truth of the Bible in this dying world, how else will they know about this great gospel of the Kingdom of

God and eternal life. The Church is the vanguard of the faith and Truth of God. The Church should show that Christ Jesus is preeminent, and our life should reflect that truth. The Holy Spirit is the power of the Believer to be rooted in Christ, to be alive in Christ, to be hidden in Christ and to be complete in Christ. The Body of Christ must turn away from all compromise, error and heresy by being the pillar and foundation of Truth. It is for this very reason that Jesus said that the Spirit of Truth will show us all things and remind us of the truth (John 14:26). Therefore, we must guard that which has been committed to the Church (1st Timothy 6:20-21). It is the Holy Spirit who helps us to grow and bear fruit in the knowledge of Christ. And know that Christ, the Lord of creation and Head of the Body, is completely sufficient for every spiritual and practical need of the Believer. True "times of refreshing comes from the presence of the Lord" (Acts 3:19).

I believe the Church has to return to true worship. And we know that in order to worship God, we must worship Him in Spirit and in Truth (John 4:24). When we worship God, He comes with His refreshing energy and hope, lifting our spirits in His direction. There must be deeper understanding based on Scripture of what it means to draw close to God by His Spirit. When surrender our hearts to Him without restriction, He gives us His heart. Our worship puts God in His rightful place in the Church and among His people where He rule and reign in royalty. Through the Holy Spirt, we find joy, hope and new life. Through the Holy Spirit, the lost will be drawn to the foot of the Cross. Through the Holy Spirit, relationships will be healed and restored. True worship is essential. It is not just being caught up in your favorite song that is sung by your favorite choir member. Singing per se is not worship. Worship was never meant to be showtime. Worship is not a performance. We are performing for one another instead of reaching out to God. Worship has to be vertical instead of horizontal. The Church has to be mindful of this because it can all become human centered. Based on Biblical principles, I believe that worship services should not be designed to attract people but instead worship services should be designed to attract the manifest presence of God through the Holy Spirit. Then He will attract people and add to the Church (Acts 2:47). The Church should seek God first not results (Matthew 6:33). Remember the gospel did not come to us in word only, but also in power and the Holy Spirit and full conviction (1st Corinthians 2:4-5). What the Church needs now more than ever is the presence and power of God the Spirit back in Churches once again. The work of God is meant to be done with the power of God. And the power of God comes from the Holy Spirit.

"If the Church will return to acknowledge that the Holy Spirit is her strength and her help, and if the Church will return to give up everything and wait upon God to be filled with the Spirit, her days of beauty and gladness will return, and we shall see the glory of God revealed among us. Nothing will help unless we come to understand that we must live every day under the power of the Holy Spirit." Andrew Murray

It is God's intent that now, through the Church, that His manifold wisdom should be made know to the rulers and authorities in the heavenly realms, according to His eternal purpose which He accomplished in Christ Jesus, Lord and Head over the Church (Ephesians 3:10-11).

The Ministry of the Holy Spirit in the Church is universal.

- He formed the Church, the Body of Christ according to Ephesians 2:19-22.
- He sanctifies the Church according to Romans 15:16.
- He comforts the Church according to Acts 9:31.
- He sends out missionaries according to Acts 8:29.
- He is Lord over the worship service according to Philippians 3:3.
- He appoints Overseers according to Acts 20:28.
- He appoints officers according to Acts 20: 17, 28.
- He anoints Overseers according to 1st Corinthians 2:4.
- He fills according to Acts 2:4.
- He baptizes according to 1st Corinthians 12:13.
- He gives gift for the work of the ministry according to 1st Corinthians 12.
- He guides to the truth according to John 16:3.

- He guides us away from sin according to Galatians 5:16.
- He disciplines according to Hebrews 12:6-11.
- He guides to purpose according to Luke 4:18.
- He guides to the will of God according to Psalm 143:10.

The primary way the Holy Spirit works in the life of the Church is through the instruction and power of the Word of God. John 14:26 states, "But the Helper, the Holy Spirit, whom the Father will send in My name, He will teach you all things, and bring to your remembrance of all things that I said to you." As Christ's Body in the earth, we must not forget that the real purpose of the Church has been etched out by God before the foundation of the world. Holy Spirit is here to remind us that the Lord's central thought and intention is to have the Church as His Body to express Himself in the earth. The Church, essentially, is for nothing other than Christ and Christ is the very life and the very nature of the Church. This is why the Church is called His Body and He is the Head. As the Church, the Body of Christ, we are to contain the life of the Head and express what the Head is. **THE CHURCH IS TO ABSOLUTELY EXPRESS CHRIST**.

The Church is God-created through the Holy Spirit. Nothing should be done in the Church without the Holy Spirit's approval. She is an educational system for discipleship and reproduction of Jesus Christ, not a religious institution unto dead works. The Church is not about ritual, routines or traditions, but about a living relationship with the True and Living God. It is not about the numerical growth but the spiritual growth. The strength of the Church is the Holy Spirit not the number of members or the size of the building. Today, appointments are done without recourse to the fullness of the Holy Spirit. Some are appointed based on their relationship with leaders in the Church. The enemy wants to change time and purpose and the Church must come into Her true identity in Christ as this Age comes to a close. If we allow Holy Spirit to have His way in our place of worship, we will experience the power of God and increase of the Lord like never before. **Selah.**

The Power of One: One Body, One Spirit. One Hope. One LORD. One Baptism. One God. One Father

"If I am delayed, you will know how people ought to conduct themselves in God's household, which is the Church of the living God, the pillar and foundation of the truth. Beyond all question, the mystery from which true godliness springs is great:

He appeared in the flesh,

Was vindicated by the Spirit,

Was seen by angels,

Was preached among the nations,

Was believed on in the world,

Was taken up in glory.

1st Timothy 3:15-16 (NIV)

Sixteen

∽

The Spirit and the (s) Word

"The Sword of the Spirit which is the Word of God."
Ephesians 6:17

"The Bible without the Holy Spirit is just literature." Prophet T. B.
Joshua

The Holy Spirit has been very instrumental and revelatory for my knowledge, understanding, growth, revelation and illumination in the Word of God from the very beginning the Lord brought me out of darkness into His marvelous light. When I found out that He is the Spirit of Truth and Teacher, I desired Him all the more. It is the Holy Ghost along with the Father and Word that bear record of heaven (1st John 5:7). It is by the revelation and illumination of Holy Spirit that I know that the Word of God can only work with the Spirit of God and vice versa. Without the Spirit the Word doesn't work and without the Word the Spirit won't work. Many Believers do not see the relationship between the Holy Spirit and the Word of God. After Jesus accomplished the Will of His Father on the Cross, God declares it to us and shows us through the words of the Bible. God so graciously placed the Grace that our Lord Jesus Christ accomplished for us in His own Word and He has sent the precious Holy Spirit to reveal it to us. The Holy Spirit is the Doorkeeper of God's Living Word. The Father has secured the finished work of Jesus in the Holy Spirit. It is the Holy Spirit that helps us receive the Word of God and when we receive the Word of God the Lord's work is applied to us. We receive God's Word by faith and Holy Spirit gives us revelation of the work of the Lord in God's Word. The work of Holy Spirit is fellowship. When the Holy Spirit comes, the Word is opened up. His Word becomes a "light to our feet and a lamp to our path" (Psalm 119:105). The entrance of His Words gives light; it gives understanding to the simple (Psalm 119:130). God is very much still at work through His Word and His Spirit today.

The Word without the Spirit is mechanical, dull and lifeless. When the Word is taught or preached without the Spirit, the results is dry and the service is mechanical, that is ritual and religious. People go through with no motivation to grow, no hunger for the Word, no satisfaction, no joy, no love, no life. People have a form of godliness. But the Word with the Spirit the Word becomes fresh and vital. He makes the difference between religion and relationship with Christ. Without the Spirit, God's Word cannot be understood. It takes God's Spirit to understand God's Word. The Holy Spirit, as the Teacher, illuminates the mind according to 1st Corinthians 2:12-13. He reveals things according to 1st Corinthians 2:10, 13 and Isaiah 40:13-14. David wrote that God's Word is a lamp to his feet and a light to his path (Psalm 119:105; 130). Illumination is the divine process whereby God causes the written revelation to be understood by the human heart. The Believer needs this illumination to help him fully grasp the saving message in God's Word. Illumination is not just for Believers, but it is also for the unsaved (John 16:8-11). An example of Holy Spirit illuminating the unsaved is on the day of Pentecost. After Peter preached about Christ and the Cross 3,000 people were save (Acts 2:36-41).

Through the Word the Holy Spirit convicts, corrects, cleanses, confirms. One of the great proofs that the Word is the divine authority of God is its unique ability to convict men and women of righteousness and of sin. In correcting, the Word serves as the rod or ruler. It is used as a standard against the which measures our beliefs. It corrects Believers when they are in honest and unintentional error. It can cleanse from wrong thoughts (Psalm 1:2), from wrong words (James 1:22-26; Psalm 119:172), and wrong actions (John 15:3). The Word confirms the truth in our hearts, our salvation (John 5:24), and confirms our forgiveness of sin (Psalm 32:5; 103:12; Isaiah 38:17).

Holy Spirit uses the Word as a sword in the spiritual armor of a Believer. It is both offensive and defensive. All Believers need training on the proper use of the Word of God by the Holy Spirit. Apostle Paul wrote in 2nd Timothy 3:16-17, "All Scripture is breathed out by God and profitable for teaching, for reproof, for correction, and for training in righteousness, that the man of God may be complete, equipped for every good work." And in Hebrews 4:12 it states, "For the Word of God is living and active, sharper than any two-edged sword, piercing to the division of soul and of spirit, of joints and of marrow, and discerning the thoughts and intentions of the heart. The Holy Spirit uses the power of the Word to save souls and then to give spiritual strength to be mature in the things of God. The Spirit and the Word gives us a life that wins.

We can absolutely trust the Holy Spirit to teach us to rightly divide the Word of Truth (2nd Timothy 2:15) because He is the Teacher and the Spirit of Truth and He will guide us into all truth. (John 16:13-15). He will never teach anything contrary to the Word of God. The Spirit and the Word always agree. All who are Born of God are given the Holy Spirit to help lead them into truth (John 14:26; 16:13). As Believers abide in Christ and obey the Word of God, the Spirit helps understand its redemptive truths and draw upon its life. Without God's living Word the Believer has nothing to stand on or stand in. The Spirit reveals that the Word is the "plum line" setting us and keeping us on the straight and narrow course. Together the Spirit and the Word is our foundation of Salvation through the Cross and the Resurrection of Christ. With the partnership and agreement of the Spirit and the Word, no one can ever discredit the Word of God, not even the Devil himself.

"In the beginning was the Word, and the Word was with God, and the Word was God. The same was in the beginning with God. All things were made by him; and without him was not anything made that was made. In him was life; and the life was the light of men...And the Word was made flesh, and dwelt among us, (and we beheld his glory, the glory as of the only begotten of the Father) full of grace and truth." (John 1:1-4, 14).

Believers are not to conformed to this the pattern of this world but be transformed by the renewing of the mind that they may prove what is that good, and acceptable and perfect will of God (Romans 12:2). Apostle Paul in essence is teaching the new creation in Christ that confession of sin in itself is not enough to empower them to automatically walk in the Spirit. The Believer must yield, submit, and surrender himself as an instrument in God's hand (Romans 6:13; James 4:7). This involves both the body (Romans 1:21; 1st Corinthians 6:20) and the mind (Romans 12:2). It is with the body that actions conceived in the mind are carried out and with the mind that they are formulated. In other words, that which is conceived in the mind is carried out in the body; thus, one's who being must be yielded, submitted, and surrendered by a decisive act of the will to God for His purpose. This consists of dedication and a willingness to whatever God commands.

The renewal of the mind is crucial in the new creation because man's mind has been darkened by sin (Romans 8:7; Colossians 1:21) and must be brought to the place where it thinks as God thinks (Ephesians 4:6-7) and through constant reading, praying and mediation on the Word of God (Psalm 119:1). This transformation will continue until we are with Christ (Philippians 1:6; 1st John 3:2). Below are some suggestions to aid in receiving the greatest benefit from reading God's Word with the aid of the Holy Spirit.

- **Prayerfully** – Ask the Spirit to meet your heart's need as your read (Psalm 119:18)

- **Thoughtfully** – Give thought to the meaning and implications of what you are reading.
- **Carefully** – Be intentional about the words and how they are used to relate to one another.
- **Repeatedly** - Repetitiveness is a good way for the Word to take root in your heart. It is a good way to digest the Word.
- **Extensively** – At times, it is wise to read large portions of the Word of God through at one sitting.
- **Regularly** – Make a habit of reading God's Word daily.
- **Faithfully** – Be consistent in your Reading.
- **Obediently** – It is essential to obey God's Word (Exodus 24:3).

With the help of the Holy Spirit God's Word:

- **Keeps** the born-again Believer from sinning (Psalm 119:11).
- **Provides** comfort in times of trouble (Psalm 119:52, 92).
- **Keeps** the mind stayed on God (Psalm 43:3).
- **Provides** daily sustenance for the spiritual life (Deuteronomy 8:3).
- **Provides** continual and ready guidance in all the situations of life (Proverbs 6:20-23).
- **Provides** the basis for formal and informal instruction (Deuteronomy 6:6-7).

"When the Spirit of truth comes, he will guide you into all truth. He will not speak on his own but will tell you what he has heard. He will tell you about the future. He will bring me glory by telling you whatever he receives from me. All that belongs to the Father is mine; this is whys I said, 'The Spirit will tell you whatever he receives from me.' John 16:13-15 (NLT). The Word of God is the instrument and channel through which the Holy Spirit does His work. The Word of God is the sword of the Spirit (Ephesians 6:17).

> *"Don't hold me to my opinions because they will probably change. But hold me to the Word of God it will never change." ~Dr. Mary J. Bryant*

Seventeen

༶

Life through the [Holy] Spirit

"And if the Spirit of Him who raised Jesus from the dead is living in you, He who raised Christ from the dead will also give life to your mortal bodies because of His Spirit who lives in you." Romans 8:11

In Romans, Apostle Paul gives the foundational teaching on the spiritual life. He gives the answers to the questions of how to be delivered from sin, how to live a balanced life under grace, and how to live the new life victoriously through the power of the Holy Spirit. In Jesus Christ, faith believers have been given the imputed righteousness that comes through the Holy Spirit who gives Christians the power to be transformed into the image and likeness of Christ and to live for Him every day. It is only through life in the [Holy] Spirit and His power that we, as born-again Believers, can bring glory to God and help to advance His Kingdom.

Because God renders His divine universal verdict, "all have sinned, and come short of the glory of God" (Romans 3:23) and all is under sin and guilty before God. In other words, all have missed the mark of attaining God's glory. Therefore, we are not able to please God and there is absolutely nothing we can do to change that on our own. But Romans 6:23 tells us that the gift of God is eternal life, and that life is through faith in Jesus Christ. This is the ONLY way for mankind to be made righteous before God and obtain redemption – through faith. Once faith is put in Christ Jesus, God declares us righteous and holy. Formerly we had come short of the glory of God, but now as born-again believers, we rejoice in the hope of the glory of God.

This is where Holy Spirit is needed. The new Believer no longer gives themselves over to the old desires before being born-again, instead they align more and more with the work of the Holy Spirit and the Word of God to become more like Jesus. In other words, they begin to live according to the Spirit and not the flesh (Romans8:4). The Holy Spirit is the One who teaches us how to live according to the Word of God. His first work is to bring us to Christ and His second work is to sanctify us. We have to cooperate with Him by offering our bodies as a living sacrifice, not conforming to the ways of this world and be transformed by the renewing of our minds (Romans 12:1-2). There has to be an appetite change to desire the pure milk of the word. There should be a craving and a thirst and hunger for God's righteousness to grow up in the fullness or completeness of salvation in Christ (1st Peter 2:2). Now be forewarned that the old nature will not leave easily. The spirit is in conflict with the flesh (old nature) and the flesh in conflict with the spirit. These two are contrary with one another (Galatians 5:17). This is why the Holy Spirit is needed because with Him dwelling in us we have power over our old nature, to subdue it and make it subject to our spirit. We must allow the [Holy] Spirit to lead us. Galatians 5:25 "If we live in the Spirit (or the Spirit lives in us), let us also walk in the Spirit." As Christians, we have to mind the things of the [Holy] Spirit if He dwells in us. If we don't have the Spirit, then we do not belong to Christ (Romans 8:9). The Truth is if Christ is in us, our body is dead to sin, and Holy Spirit is Lord over our spirits as we live to all righteousness (2nd Corinthians 5:17-18; Romans 8:10). Therefore, the flesh has no more control over us. We, therefore, are commanded to put to death the practices of the flesh by the [H0ly] Spirit (Romans 8:13).

Life through the Spirit is a victorious life. Instead of fighting for victory, we fight from victory. Because Christ Himself has given us the victory. This victory allows Christians to have freedom in Jesus to produce the fruits of righteousness through a Spirit-led lifestyle. The Book of Galatians records the power, "Walk in the Spirit" (Galatians 5:16) and the results, "the fruit of the Spirit" (Galatians 5:22) of that freedom. I believe Apostle Paul wrote the Christian's declaration of independence: It is the power of the Holy Spirit empowers the Christian to enjoy freedom within the law of love. And we know that faith works by love (Galatians 5:6).

Why is faith so important? First, our salvation begins with faith and our maturity in Christ must continue in faith. "Start with faith, continue with faith, and end with faith." (Dr. Mary J. Bryant). This faith has to release the belief that we are set free of the bondage of sin because of the power of the Holy Spirit living in us. Our freedom in Christ does not give us an excuse to indulge in the deeds or practices of the flesh, but rather freedom in Christ provides the privilege of bearing the fruit of the Spirit by walking in dependence upon Him. I cannot repeat this enough. We need Holy Spirit to live this new life in victory by putting faith in Jesus Christ. And we know that when we are living a victorious life, we seek to please God in every aspect of our life. The Holy Spirit gives us the conviction and trust we need to help us stand strong against the evil temptations of this world (Romans 1:17; 1st Corinthians 10:13).

In the eighth chapter of Romans Apostle Paul gives us a breakdown of the Holy Spirit in the born-again Believer's life. He tells us that spiritual life, freedom from condemnation, victory over sin and fellowship with God come through union with Christ Jesus by the indwelling Holy Spirit. 1) The [Holy] Spirit delivers us from the power of the flesh, 2) the [Holy] Spirit gives us sonship, 3) the Spirit assures us of the future glory, and 4) the [Holy] Spirit assures of the final victory. When we are delivered from the power of the flesh, from verses 1-11, it confirms that "there is therefore now no condemnation to them which are in Christ Jesus, who walk not after the flesh but after the Spirit. We have the "law of the Spirit of life" which operates in us. This operation is not automatic, but we must surrender and commit to obeying the Spirit. With the indwelling and leading of Holy Spirit we have a new "operating system" for this brand-new life in Christ. We no longer operate according to this world system or our flesh (old nature). Instead, the operation of the Holy Spirit empowers us to live lives of righteousness. For from faith-to-faith righteousness is revealed (Romans :17). In these first 11 verses, Paul gives us the description of two groups of people. The first group according to the sinful nature and the second group lives according to the Spirit. In other words, he is saying that the sinful nature is occupied with its desires, thoughts, emotions, and lust (also see Galatians 5:19-21). On the other hand, those who live "in accordance with the Spirit" seek and submit to the Spirit's leading, instruction, and command to focus their attention, thoughts, energy, and will on the things of God. Their minds are set on things above (Colossians 3:2). It is a consciously continuous living in God's presence, trusting Him to give us the help and grace we need to accomplish His will in and through us. We know that the Bible tells us that if we live according to the sinful nature, we "cannot please God" (Romans 8:8). Then from verses 12 – 17 tells us that we owe the flesh nothing. Although We are no longer in debt to the flesh, as believers we must continually decide whether we will surrender to sinful desires or to the demands of the divine nature in which we participate (Galatians 5:16, 18; 2nd Peter 1:4).

Often times the message of Romans chapter 7 is not rightly divided. It is preached as we as weak when it comes to sin and there is nothing, we can do about it. So, because we are powerless to sin, we can keep on sinning. However, I beg to differ, I believe Apostle Paul is painting a picture of the unregenerated person who is conscious of his or her inability to live a life that pleases God. It shows the picture of the conflict between someone who struggles in their own effort against the power of sin. Thus no one can attain justification or sanctification by one's attempt to resist sin and obey God. Anyone who tries to obey God's commands without the saving grace of Christ will find out that they are incapable of accomplishing this no matter how good the intentions are. Why? Because that person is not their own master but evil and sin rule over them. In other words, evil and sin are masters over them (Romans 7:15-21) and are prisoners of the law of sin (vs. 23). Every effort of trying to live a life free from the bondage of sin and immorality will be useless if one is not truly born again, reconciled to God, redeemed from Satan's power and made new creatures in Christ, living a renewed life in the Spirit (John 3:3; Romans 8; 2nd Corinthians 5:17).

The unregenerated person will be taken prisoner after maintaining a losing battle with sin and immorality (Romans 7:23). It is believed by the early church that there were seven sin roots in the human heart: pride, covetousness, lust, envy, gluttony (indulgence of the flesh), anger and sloth. The sinful state of the unregenerated heart is wretched and apart from the power of the cross and the Spirit of Christ within. Only in Christ will God provide the way out of temptation, so that one can stand up under it (1st Corinthians 10:13). Therefore, as a Christian, the conflict handled in union with Christ and the Holy Spirit against the power of sin (Galatians 5:16-18).

Again, this Chapter Seven of Romans is explaining the picture of the pre-conversion before conversion. In verse 14 it states, "We know that law is spiritual; but I am unspiritual." Paul is actually pointing to the insufficiency of the law to redeem us apart from grace, not the insufficiency of the gospel of grace to redeem and deliver us from sin's power (Romans 6:15-18). But the person in Chapter Seven is still under the power of the sinful nature. The expression "sold as a slave to sin" is saying "bondage to sin's power". Thus, those who are controlled by the sinful nature are bearing fruit for death and if one lives according to the sinful nature, will die (Galatians 5:19-21). In other words, this chapter is not referring to a believer in Christ, since Christ, by the ransom of His Blood, has redeemed us from the power of sin and declares that sin no longer has dominion or power over the believer in Christ (Matthew 20:28; Romans 6:14). What the Bible means by ransom is a price paid to obtain the freedom of others. In the redemptive work of Christ and the Cross, His death is the sufficient price paid for the release of humanity from sin's dominion. It is the release from condemnation (Romans 3:25-26). It is the release from sin (Ephesians 1:7) and death (Romans 8:2). In fact, the name Jesus means "He will save His people form their sins (Matthew 1:21). Additionally, the indwelling presence of the Holy Spirit (Romans 8) does not leave believers in a state of bondage and slavery to sin's power. In other words, through Christ Jesus the law of the Spirit of life sets believers free from the law of sin (Romans 8:2). Those who live according to the Spirit is not obligated to live according to the sinful nature any longer.

As the Apostle moves on to further discuss life through the Spirit in Chapter Eight in Romans, He teaches us that spiritual life, freedom from condemnation, victory over sin and fellowship with God come through union with Christ by the indwelling Holy Spirit. It is not just enough to have the Spirit dwell in us, but He has to lead us, and we have to follow Him. Because by the Holy Spirit we are delivered from sin's power. In verse two, it teaches that through Christ Jesus, the law of the Spirit of life has set us free from the law of the sin and death. In other words, the law of the Spirit of life is the regulating, activating power and life of the Holy Spirit working in our hearts as born-again believers. Again, once the Holy Spirit comes into our hearts, we much yield and submit to Him so that He will be in full operation within. Once that happens, the Believer has a new operating system with Dunamis Power (which is not supernatural) to overcome sin. It is the Holy Spirit working within that allows us to live a life of righteousness.

In Chapter Five, the Apostle describes two kinds of people; those who live according to the sinful nature and those who live according to the Spirit. In describes those who live by the sinful have their minds and is occupied with its desires, thoughts, emotions and physical gratification: sexual immorality, adultery, hatred, selfish ambition, outbursts of anger, and etc. (Galatians 5:19-21). Those who live according to the Spirit seeks and submits to the Holy Spirit's direction and empowerment and focuses on their thoughts and desires on the things of God Or things above (Colossians 3:2). Galatians list the Fruit of the Spirit: love, joy, peace, forbearance, kindness, goodness, faithfulness, gentleness and self-control. In other words, it is to live consciously at all times in God's presence, trusting Him to give us the power and the grace we need to accomplish His will in and through us (Philippians 2:13). Know that anyone who is controlled by the sinful nature cannot please God (Romans 8:8). Then Paul wrote in verse 9 that if anyone has the Spirit of God living in them, they are not controlled by the sinful nature. For if Christ is in us, our body is dead because of sin, yet our spirit is alive because of righteousness (Romans 8:11). There is no compromise to God's Word. "If you live according to the sinful nature, you will die (spiritually) but if by the Spirit you put to death the misdeeds of the body, you will live [now and eternally] (Romans 8:13). Lay hold of the Truth: If anyone does not have the Spirit of Christ, he/she does not belong to Christ (Romans 8:9).

Apostle also lets us know that through the life in the Spirit, He testifies with our spirit that we are God's children (Romans 8:16). Holy Spirit brings the truth to our heart (spirit) that Christ loves us and lives for us in heaven as Mediator (Hebrews 7:25). The Holy Spirit also teaches that we are loved by the Father as His adopted children. In fact, God loves us just as He loves Jesus, His Son (John 14:21, 23; 17:23)). The life through the Spirit creates in us the love and confidence by which we cry Abba Father (Romans 8:15). It is the Holy Spirit Himself who intercedes on our behalf and helps us in our weakness. He does this because we don't know what we should pray for (Romans8:26). In verse 27, it states, "And he who searches our hearts knows the mind of the Spirit, because the Spirit intercedes for the saints in accordance with God's will." We are told that Jesus will baptize with the Holy Spirit and fire (Matthew 3:11; Acts 2:3-4). (I go into more detail about the baptism of the Holy Spirit in the chapter: Jesus and the Holy Spirit).

As True Believers, we must continually decide whether we will surrender to sinful nature or the Spirit. Why? Because it is a continual warfare against the spiritual life and sin is always striving to regain control of us. The Christian life without the power of the Holy Ghost is a life of failure. Without our continual yielding and submitting to the Holy Spirit's guidance and conviction of sin, sin will continue to be "stumbling blocks" causing us to continue to think that sin has power over us, which is a lie from the enemy. But the Christian's true reality is that with God's Spirit, we have the power over sin and live a life pleasing to God. Because of the Gift of Holy Spirit, Born-again faith believers now have a new power source to live a Godly life. Life through the Spirit is the power source activated within. Each of us must choose to yield, submit and rely on this power source.

Seven Key Ministries of Holy Spirit in the life of the believer:

1. Walk according to the Spirit (Romans 8:2-4)
2. Set your mind on the things of the Spirit (Romans 8:5-8)
3. Put to death the deeds of the body by the Spirit (Romans 8:5-8)
4. Be led by the Spirit (Romans 8:14)
5. Know the Fatherhood of God by the Spirit (Romans 8:15-17)
6. Hope in the Spirit (Romans 8:23-25)
7. Pray in the Spirt (Romans 8:26-27)

Believe by faith that in life through the Spirit:

1. We are not under divine condemnation.
2. We are not in bondage to the flesh.
3. We are indwelt by the Holy Spirit.
4. We belong to Christ Jesus.
5. We are spiritually alive in Christ Jesus.
6. We are children of God.
7. We are adopted into God's heavenly family.
8. We are covered in prayer and love by Holy Spirit.

Eighteen

༄

Walking in the [Holy] Spirit

Confession. Yielding. Filling

"I say then: Walk in the Spirit, and you shall not fulfill the lust of the flesh."
Galatians 5:16

The Believer's life is described as walking in the Spirit. Walking in the Spirit best represents the step-by-step and moment-by-moment character of the new life in Christ led by Holy Spirit. It is living by the divine spiritual power of God by yielding and surrendering our will for His will. Walking in the Spirit involves confession of sin, yielding to God, and being filled with or controlled by Holy Spirit. It is not us "catching" the Holy Spirit, but it is giving complete control to Him. As Believers we need Holy Spirit for this journey here on Earth. God gives the Holy Spirit without limit (John 3:34).

Jesus, Himself, needed Holy Spirit in His earthly ministry. We read this in the Gospel according to John as an account of John the Baptizer. When John, Prophet of the Most High God, baptized Jesus in the Jordan River, He testified by saying that he saw the [Holy] Spirit descending from heaven like a dove, and it rested and remained upon Jesus (John 1:32-33; Mark 1:9-10). In Mark's account of the gospel, he makes mention that immediately after Jesus was baptized, Holy Spirit drove Him into the wilderness (1:12). During Jesus's earthly ministry, He was 100% God, and He was 100% human, but He needed Holy Spirit to do the will of the Father. His humanity needed Holy Spirit to be able to commune with the Father. Through the Spirit, Jesus was always connected with heaven. Remember Jesus was conceived by Holy Spirit (Matthew 1:18-20; Luke 1:35). The Prophet Isaiah also spoke of Jesus as the coming Messiah as One endowed with the Spirit (Isaiah 42:1; 61:1). Holy Spirit took a prominent role in the life of Jesus. He received the Spirit without measure (John 3:34). Christ was even resurrected by Holy Spirit (Romans 8:11). It was the authority of Holy Spirit, the Spirit of holiness, to declare Jesus the Son of God (Romans 1:4; 1 Timothy 3:16; 1st Peter 3:18).

So, what does this means for Believers? It means that the same Spirit that was on Jesus is the same Spirit we need to accomplish what we cannot accomplish on our own. Jesus gave us the same power and authority He used on earth to do the Father's will. Thus, the Spirit's ministry comes to us from God (Acts 2:33). As He [Jesus] walked depending on Holy Spirit so does Believers in Christ need to depend on Him. In fact, Jesus promised the disciples that He was going to send another Comforter [another, like Jesus] (John 14:16). The Greek word used for Comforter is Parakletos which literally means "one called alongside to help." [Strong's #3875]. This word is used 5 times in the Bible (John 14:16, 14:26, 15:26, 16:7; 1st John 2:1). The ministry of Holy Spirit has been promised to all who put their faith in Jesus. In this new life, Jesus has not abandoned us or left us as orphans (John 14:18), but He has poured out on us and in us the very same [Holy] Spirit through whom He lived perfectly, died sacrificially, and rose on the third day, victoriously. Jesus told the disciples then as well as disciples now in John 16:13-15 "But when the truth-giving Spirit comes, He will unveil the reality of every truth within you. He won't speak His own message, but only what He hears the Father, and He will reveal prophetically to you what is to come. He will glorify Me on the Earth, for He will receive from Me what is Mine and reveal it to you. Everything that belongs to the Father belongs to me – that's why

I say that the Divine Encourager will receive what is Mine and reveal it to you (TPT). Let me note here that the Greek word for "truth" is "reality" not doctrine. It is the application of the truth that matters, not just a superficial knowledge. Holy Spirit plants what is Jesus' and shows it to us. He reveals it and illuminates it.

I especially love how Apostle Paul expresses the life through the Spirit in Romans Chapter 8. In this Chapter, Paul explains that the spiritual life, freedom from condemnation, victory over sin and fellowship with God come through union with Christ by the indwelling of the Holy Spirit. Receiving and walking by the Spirit is the only way to be delivered from the power of sin. It is the law of the Spirit of Life that sets us free from the law of sin and death (Romans 8:1). The law of the Spirit comes into full operation as Believers commit themselves to obey Holy Spirit (Romans 8:4-5 13-14). The Holy Spirit empowers Believers to live righteous lives through the operation of grace and obedience to God's law.

Paul describes two classes of people in the eighth Chapter of Romans. There are those who live according to the sinful nature and those who live according to the Spirit. He described those who live according to the sinful nature as those who are occupied with the old nature's desires, thoughts, emotions physical gratification (Romans 8:4-14). He described those who live according to the Spirit as those who see and submit to the Holy Spirit's leading and to focus one's thoughts, energy and ways on the things of God. In other words, it is to live consciously and consistently in the presence of God, trusting Him to give them the grace that is needed to accomplish His will in and through them. The sinful nature and the new nature are in conflict with each other. Anyone who calls himself a Christian and still follow the sinful nature shuts themselves out of the Kingdom of God. Some deceive themselves in thinking that even if they broke fellowship with Christ by their sinful lifestyle, their salvation and inheritance in God's Kingdom is still secure. However, spiritual death is the inevitable consequences of habitual sinning (Romans 8:13). One who has put faith in Jesus and claim to know God in a saving relationship cannot be indifferent to God's will and His commands and disobey them (John 17:3). Thus, to attempt to be justified through faith in Christ Jesus without a commitment to follow Him as Lord will lead to doom and failure (Matthew 16:24). Listen, those who are truly born of God cannot make sin their way of life. Why? Because God's life cannot exist in those who make a practice or habit of sinning (1st John 1:5-7; 2:3-11, 15-17, 24-29; 3:6-24; 4:7-8, 20). Regeneration (new birth) produces spiritual life that results in an ever-present fellowship with God. Therefore, for people to have God's life in them (Born for God) and habitually sin is a spiritual contradiction. It goes against what the Bible teaches. Let me note that Some Believers may backslide or lapse from God's way, but they will not continue in sin deliberately as a lifestyle (1st John 3:6, 10). However, at the same time, ALL Believers can live moment by moment free from the sinful nature or power of sin. How? By faith that God's very life, Spirit and nature along with the indwelling Christ, the power of the Holy Spirit and the written Word (1st John 5:4, 11-12; John 15:4; 2nd Peter 1:4; 1st Thessalonians 2:10) lives in them. Apostle Paul reiterates this teaching in Galatians 21 and Ephesians 5:5-6. Remember there is no true salvation without the regenerating and sanctifying work of the Holy Spirit (1st Corinthians 6:11).

Believers must also set their minds on the things of the Spirit. Likewise, in the renewing of the mind or the emptying of the mind, it should be filled with spiritual things that only can be given by Holy Spirit. Paul wrote in Galatians 5:22-23 what being filled with spiritual things look like. We must have the fruit of the Spirit (love, joy, peace, long-suffering, gentleness, goodness, faith, meekness, and temperance) to have the character of Christ to the fullest and to please God. In Verse 3 of Romans 8, we are told to put to death the deeds of the body by the Spirit. Simply put Believers need HELP to put to death our old nature because it is not just saying no to sinning, but it is living as one who has died to every form of lawlessness (Colossians 3:5). Regeneration calls for the Believer to move on and leave the old self behind and not stay stuck in sin. The power of saying "no" must be done by Holy Spirit and our willingness to obey Him. James teaches that being humbly submitted to God, we can resist the devil and he will flee from us (James 4:7). Going on to verse 14, Believers are told to be led by the Spirit. Because those led by the Spirit are God's children (Romans 8:14). When Holy Spirit leads us, we will put to death the deeds of the body and live (vs. 13). He always leads Believers in the path of righteousness; therefore, the new Believer is under no obligation to the flesh. Galatians 5 teaches us life by the Spirit. It is walking and living by the Spirit Believers will not gratify the desires of the sinful nature (vs. 16). Yet, if we ignore the Spirit's leading and engage in evil practices of the sinful nature, we will not inherit the Kingdom of God. The Bible explicitly teaches that sinful nature (Old nature) desires what is contrary to the Spirit and the Spirit what is contrary to the sinful nature (Galatians 1:17). Apostle Paul emphasizes the necessity for continual warfare against all that is contrary to God. As Believers, we must continually decide whether we will surrender to sinful desires or to the demands of the divine nature, the new nature. To fail to put to death the misdeeds of the body is spiritual death. The life of the God that we received at the new birth can be extinguished in the soul who refuses to put to death by the Spirit the misdeeds of the body.

The Holy Spirit lives in the child of God in order to lead him to think, speak and act according to God's Word. When we consistently put to death the misdeeds of the body, we know that Holy Spirit is leading us. Holy Spirit always leads the Believer to follow the will of God. We are kept under grace through Holy Spirit. A Spirit-led lifestyle is freedom in Christ to produce the fruits of righteousness. Now that Believers have a new standing with God through Christ, we have been adopted into His Royal family. Romans 8:15-17 tells us that we have received the Spirit of adoption. This is a spiritual truth and reality that Believers cannot know on their own, but the Spirit bears witness with their spirit that they are children of God. This means that Believers are joint heir with Christ. It is the Holy Spirit that helps Believer cry Abba Father. Believers must rely on Holy Spirit in all spiritual matters.

Walking in the Spirit also gives the Believer hope for the future. Romans 8:22-25 shares how Believers groan inwardly waiting for the redemption of their bodies. In these verses, it is precisely the presence of the Spirit within Believers that causes suffering. This suffering is the longing for final redemption in the midst of a fallen world. So, the hope we receive from Holy Spirit is that He reminds us of the overwhelming contrast between those glorious things the Father has prepared for them and this sinful world.

Meanwhile, when Believers become tired and weary, it is Holy Spirit that is right alongside them to help them along. The last two verses, 26-27, shows how walking in the Spirit allows Believers to pray in the Spirit. These verses are so rich and helpful in the Believer's life in the Spirit. Prayer is essential to the Believer. We even read where the disciples asked Jesus to teach them to pray (Luke 11:1-14; Matthew 6:9-15). Believers must also request to be taught to pray. It is Holy Spirit who joins with Believers to help when there is a struggle in knowing how to pray and what to pray. Holy Spirit searches the heart and knows the mind-set of the person praying. The objective for answered prayers is to pray according to the will of God and Holy Spirit knows the will of God. In other words, Holy Spirit is moving us to pray, and He is presenting the prayers that He is leading us to pray to the Father in the name of the Lord Jesus.

If Believers want to live the life Jesus promised us and came to give us, then we must walk in the Spirit. Holy Spirit is the One who brings God's plan to realty and fulfillment. He is the executor of God's nature and is the source of the new birth. He conforms us to the nature of Jesus. There is no point in becoming born-again and not walk in the Spirit for God is Spirit. The Bible teaches that the carnal mind is enmity against God and those who are in the human nature (flesh) cannot please God (Romans 8:7-8). Confession, yielding, and filling are three prerequisites to walking in the Spirit. Walking in the Spirit is just living a life in the Spirit and by the Spirit. Galatians 5:16-25 teaches this about walking in the Spirit.

> *So I say, walk by the Spirit, and you will not gratify the desires of the flesh. For the flesh desires what is contrary to the Spirit, and the Spirit what is contrary to the flesh. They are in conflict with each other, so that you are not to do whatever you want. But if*

you are led by the Spirit, you are not under the law. The acts of the flesh are obvious: sexual immorality, impurity and debauchery; idolatry and witchcraft; hatred, discord, jealousy, fits of rage, selfish ambition, dissensions, factions and envy; drunkenness, orgies, and the like. I warn you, as I did before, that those who live like this will not inherit the kingdom of God. But the fruit of the Spirit is love, joy, peace, forbearance, kindness, goodness, faithfulness, gentleness and self-control. Against such things there is no law. Those who belong to Christ Jesus have crucified the flesh with its passions and desires. Since we live by the Spirit, let us keep in step with the Spirit. Let us not become conceited, provoking and envying each other.

Holy Spirit is one of God's most precious gifts to Believers. He is given to empower each Believer in the new life in Christ, but the power of Holy Spirit can be turned off or ignored. Only those individuals who agree to walk in Him have access to the ministry of Holy Spirit. I challenge each of us to allow the leading of Holy Spirit to be the normal lifestyle as children of the Most High God. If you are not yet walking in the Spirit, start today and allow Him to do the will of God in your life.

Confession

"If we confess our sins, He is faithful and just to forgive us our sins and cleanse us from all unrighteousness."

1ˢᵗ John 1:9

The definition for confession that will be used is an acknowledgment of sins to God (Leviticus 16:21; Ezra 9:5-15; Daniel 9:3-12). The Bible has at least 100 verses of confession of sin. In the Bible, we see confession linked to both our faith and our sins. Both are declarations of what God has said and we repeat what God said to be true and reliable. Our confession of faith means we publicly declare our belief in Jesus Christ. When we confess our sins, we are agreeing with what God has said. So, when God said to confess your sin, then we know that we have sinned. We sin against God and God alone. Confession is an act of humility and need. Through confession, we make known our depravity to the infinite Holy God. Without the help of Holy Spirit, we would not be able to recognize that we are sinners (before the new birth). Once the revelation and illumination come by Holy Spirit to see our depraved condition, we are given the chance to confess and turn from and turn to God in faith in Jesus.

Confession is necessary in starting the salvation process. Sin separates people from God. Sin must be confessed to restore fellowship with a Holy God. With a godly sorrow, confession is made to a forgiving God. This type of confession is more than just acknowledging the sin or saying you are sorry, but it requires an attitude of sorrow for the sin and a willingness to turn from it and receive mercy. Mercy is given to sinners, so they don't get what they deserve. In God's mercy, He doesn't point fingers at you, but He pardons you. Through this act, the person gets to see their nature apart from God. Holy Spirit bears witness with the spirit to show the dead state it is in and without the rebirth of the spirit it cannot live again.

Here's the thing, the Bible teaches that all peoples need to have their sins forgiven so they can receive eternal salvation. Salvation comes in knowing that forgiveness is needed and receiving the forgiveness that has been already provided through the blood of Jesus Christ. In First John 3:4 we are taught that sin is transgression/disobedience of/to God's law. All of humanity has committed this sin. God puts all under this same sin (Romans 3:23) and all need to be justified (forgiven) by His grace through the redemption that is in Christ Jesus (Romans 3:24). In other words, without forgiveness there is no hope for eternal life.

The expression, "confession is good for the soul" is a true statement. Confession opens the way to connecting with the Lover and Bishop of the soul. I believe just as Jesus is the mediator between God and man, Holy Spirit is the mediator between God Father and God Son. Holy Spirit reveals God thoughts, teaches, and guides Believers into all truth and knowledge of what is to come. Through Him Believers are saved, filled, sealed, and sanctified. Yes, without Holy Spirit we could not experience union and unity with God. We should all endeavor to make Him our best friend.

Yielding

"I Beseech you therefore, brethren, by the mercies of God, that ye present your bodies a living sacrifice, holy, acceptable unto God, which is your reasonable service."

Romans 12:1

Confession is not enough to enable the Believer to automatically walk in the Spirit. Therefore, there must be a yielding. The Believer must become a yielded instrument for God's service. This involves both the mind (Romans 12:2) and the body (1st Corinthians 6:20). The mind and body must be yielded and surrendered because it is with the body that actions are conceived in the mind are carried out. In other words, that which is conceived in the mind is carried out in the body. Therefore, the whole being must be presented by a decisive act of the will to God for His service. Let me caution here that yielding must not be thought of simply as a willingness to do some specific thing. Rather, it consists of dedication by a person to walk in the Spirit and do whatever God commands.

Yielding leads to dedication and separation. Romans 12:2 teaches not to be conformed to this world [stop conforming yourselves]. Why? Because this world is completely opposed to God and the Believer cannot lusts for the world and do the will of God at the same time. The term "world" is often used to describe the community of sinful humanity that possesses a spirit of rebellion against God. The Apostle John wrote in First John 2:15, "Love not the world, neither the things that are in the world. If any man loves the world, the love of the Father is not in him." Because of its opposition to God, the world values those things which are contrary to God's will: "the lust of the flesh, and the lust of the eyes, and the pride of life" (1st John 2:16; 1st John 5:19). There must be a decision to separate from the world system and not be fashioned after it. The Believer must be separated in spirit, thought, values, and actions according to the world's standard. Yielding must be by faith because it is impossible to please God without faith (Hebrew 11:6).

Yielding also includes transformation of the mind. This is a lifetime process of renewing the mind. Why? Because the mind has been darkened by sin (Romans 8:7; Colossians1:21) and must be brought to the place where it thinks as God thinks (Ephesians 4:23). The Believer is to have the mind of Christ (1st Corinthians 2:16; Philippians 2:5). The mind matters in the struggle between the spirit and the flesh. That is why James 4:7-8 teaches to submit to God and resist the devil and he will flee from you.

Galatians 5:16-26 from the Passion Translation really sums up why the Believer should yield to Holy Spirit. *"As you yield freely and fully to the dynamic life and power of the Holy Spirit, you will abandon the cravings of your self-life. For your self-life craves the things that offend the Holy Spirit and hinder him from living free within you! And the Holy Spirit's intense cravings hinder your old self-life from dominating you! So then, the two incompatible and conflicting forces within you are your self-life of the flesh and the new creation life of the Spirit. But when you are brought into the full freedom of the Spirit of grace, you will no longer be living under the domination of the law but soaring above it! The cravings of the self-life are obvious: Sexual immorality, lustful thoughts, pornography, chasing after things instead of God, manipulating others, hatred of those who get in your way, senseless arguments, resentment when others are favored, temper tantrums, angry quarrels, only thinking of yourself, being in love with your own opinions, being envious of the blessings of others, murder, uncontrolled addictions, wild parties, and all other similar behavior. Haven't I already warned you that those who use their "freedom" for these things will not inherit the kingdom realm of God! But the fruit produced by the Holy Spirit within you is divine love in all its varied expressions: joy that over-flows, peace that subdues, patience that endures, kindness in action, a life full of virtue, faith that prevails, gentleness of heart, and strength of spirit. Never set the law above these qualities, for they are meant to be limitless. Keep in mind that we who belong to Jesus, the Anointed One, have already experienced crucifixion. For everything connected with our self-life was put to death on the cross and crucified with Messiah. We must live in the Holy Spirit and follow him. So, may we never be arrogant, or look down on another, for each of us is an original. We must forsake all jealousy that diminishes the value of others." Selah.*

Filling

"And be not drunk with wine, wherein is excess; but be filled with the Spirit;"
Ephesians 5:18

After the Believer has confessed and yielded to the Spirit by faith, now there can come the filling process. First, the indwelling of the Spirit and the filling of the Spirit are different. The indwelling of the Spirit is for all Born again Believers. However, the filling of the Spirit is a repeated ex-perience as with the example of the first century Believers, who were filled more than once (Acts 2:4; 4:31). Filling is a command to obeyed, not an option. When a Believer is filled with the Spirit, he is to be controlled by the Spirit, thus walking in the Spirit. Therefore, this is crucial to success-fully living the new life.

An important truth to realize is that following the outpouring at Pentecost, the power and the filling of the Holy Spirit became available to all who accept Jesus Christ and born of the Spirit (John 3:3-8). Essentially, the filling of the Spirit, depends on our relationship with the Lord. When we yield ourselves by faith to the control of the Holy Spirit, there is evidence of the Spirit filled life both internally and externally. The filling is conditional and not automatic, but it requires a desire for an internal relationship between Holy Spirit and the person. Remember Jesus taught about praying by asking, seeking, and knocking. He said that everyone who asks will receive, everyone who seeks will find and everyone who knocks will have the door open. Then Jesus said if evil fathers know how to give good gifts, how much more does the Heavenly Father will give His children the filling of Holy Spirit (Luke 11:9-13). God gives us the greater gift. He always gives us Himself through the Holy Spirit to be with us in all circumstances. There must be obedience to God's commands that will allow the Spirit to freely work in us.

Believers must recognize they need to be filled with Holy Spirit in this regenerated lifestyle. To be filled with the Spirit implies freedom for Him to occupy every part of the Believer's life. Jesus said in John 7:37-38, "If any man thirst, let him come unto me, and drink. He that believeth on me, as the scripture hath said, out of his belly shall flow rivers of living water." There has to be a desire (thirst), repentance (turn, come to Me), receiving of God's offer of Holy Spirit (drink), and acting on the basis of faith in the Word of God (belief in Jesus). In other words, being filled by the Spirit is not getting more of Him but Him getting more of the Believer. It is not a feeling or an emotional experience, but rather, the yielding of the Believer's life to God's will and obedience to God's Word.

Remember Walking in the Spirit requires confession and yielding all in obedience and desire to be filled with the Spirit and this takes faith. "Those who live according to the Spirit set their minds on the things of the Spirit" (Romans 8:5). We drink Holy Spirit by setting our minds on the things of His. What that looks like is set forth in Colossians 3:1-2. Holy Spirit minds spiritual things from the Father. In other words, drinking Holy Spirit means seeking the things of the Spirit, directing your attention to the things of the Spirit, and being devoted to the things of the Spirit. I always say that when we mind what matters to God, God minds what matters to us. God has given the ministry of the Holy Spirit for the life of the Believer to have access to the Kingdom Realm on earth. The key to rightly living this life is being controlled by Holy Spirit, who provides energy for walking worthy of the calling with which we have been called (Ephesians 4:1). Humility, love, unity, light, and wisdom cannot be manifested unless we are walking in the Spirit. The walking in the Spirit is a profound reality in the Believer's life that changes and transforms our life. So, be filled with the Spirit, continually. Renew your commitment to being Spirit-filled and Spirit-led. ***Confession. Yielding. Filling. Always remember that the flesh is still in us, but we are not in the flesh.***

Some Biblical Evidence of the filling of the Holy Spirit

- Holy Spirit filled Bezaleel according to Exodus 31:2
- He filled Jesus according to Luke 4:1
- Holy Spirit filled John the Baptist according to Luke 1:15, 60
- Holy Spirit filled Elizabeth according to Luke 1:41
- Holy Spirit filled Zacharias according to Luke 1:67
- Holy Spirit filled the followers of Jesus according to Acts 2:1-4
- Holy Spirit filled Peter according to Acts 4:8
- Holy Spirit filled Stephen according to Acts 7:55
- Holy Spirit filled Barnabas according to Acts 11:22, 24
- Holy Spirit filled Paul according to Acts 13:9
- Holy Spirit filled certain disciples according to Acts 13:52

Nineteen

༄

Love Poured Out by the Holy Spirit

*"...because God's love has been poured out into our hearts through the Holy Spirit, who has been given to us. "*Romans 5:5 (NIV)

Generally, when a person is teaching on love, they will list the four unique forms of love (some say they are eight). They would list Eros, Storge, Philia, and Agape. For this chapter we will focus on Agape (Uh-GAH-Pay). Most everyone knows that this love is the highest of the four types of love in the Bible. This term defines God's divine, immeasurable, incomparable, perfect, and unconditional love for His human creation. This love is sacrificial. God demonstrated this through death of Jesus Christ. True love is primarily an action. "For God so loved the world, that he gave his only Son... (John 3:16). Though love is one of the most powerful emotions we can experience on a human level, the Christian's love is the truest test of genuine faith because "faith works by love" (Galatians 5:6). Love is the driving force behind faith. It is said that fear is the opposite of faith, but I believe that unbelief is the opposite of faith, and the opposite of fear is love. When we struggle to believe that God's promises will come to pass, it is unbelief, and the root of unbelief is a lack of love. When we seek a greater revelation of God's love for us, then faith would come naturally. The Word of God consistently holds to the truth that a person is saved through faith (Galatians 2:15-16; Romans 3:22; Ephesians 2:8-9). And in Galatians 5;6, Apostle Paul defines the exact nature of that faith. The faith we are given is a saving faith that is a living faith in a living Savior, a faith so vital that it cannot avoid expressing itself in love-motivated deeds. The faith that does not sincerely love and obey Christ (1st John 2:3; 5:3), does not show a real concern for the advancement of God's Kingdom (Matthew 12:28) and actively submit to God and resist sin and the world (James 4:7; Galatians 6:16-17) does not qualify as saving faith (James 2:14-16).

First Corinthians 13 is commonly known as the "love chapter" because it expresses love as the greatest of the three that remain (faith, hope and love). Apostle Paul is emphasizing that the functioning of the spiritual gifts without having God's love is unprofitable (vv. 1-3). The "most excellent way" (1st Corinthians 12:31) is not love instead of the gifts, but rather the exercise of spiritual gifts in love (vv.4-8). Love MUST be the governing principle of all spiritual manifestations. This chapter describes love in action not just as an emotion (13:4-7). It includes the various aspects of love that characterize God the Father, Son and Holy Spirit. As Believers, we must earnestly and eagerly seek to grow in this kind of love. Thus, it is very clear that God exalts love over ministry, faith or spiritual gifts. Therefore, the greatest in the Kingdom of God will be those of us who are great in inner goodness and who demonstrate genuine love for God and people.

It is Jesus who calls us to a life of holy intimacy and personal devotion to Him. This is only possible because of God's love for us (1st John 4:19), which He poured into our hearts by the Holy Spirit (Romans 5:5). How did God demonstrate His love for us? He demonstrated His perfect love through Christ's dying for us while we were still sinners (Romans 5:8). Therefore, we are to remain in the love of Jesus by pursuing spiritual intimacy and communion with, and by obeying His commands, just as He did with the Father (John 15:9-10). This is why Jesus commanded

His disciples in John 13:34 to love one another. "A new command I give you: Love one another. As I have loved you, so you must love one another." The love Jesus is commanding is the agape love. Agape love is the distinguishing mark of His followers (1st John 3:23; 4:7-21). It is love that is basically a self-giving and sacrificial love that seeks the good of another (1st John 4:9-10). It is love characterized by a devoted concern that sacrificially seeks to promote the highest good of our brothers and sisters in Christ. Since we are God's children, we must walk in love. It is not an option; it is a command by Jesus Himself. In fact, John wrote that if we do not love, we do not know God. Thus, this love is practical. It is more than mere words, but action. It is a giving love without expecting anything in return. It is an "in spite of" love. Our belief in Christ should be in the practice of love for each other, which in turn produces joy and confidence before God. Regeneration is shown in righteousness (1st John 2:29-3:10) is manifested in love (1st John 3:10-23). When we obey the command to love one another, there is a mutual abiding of the believer in God and God in the believer that produces a divine and human fellowship that testifies to and reflects the reality of the incarnation (1st John 7-16). Profession without practice is useless. Because the world needs to see our love one for another to believe that we are disciples of Jesus. More importantly that Jesus Christ is the Redeemer that Reconciles us back to God.

Love is the most powerful force in the world of human beings and hate is just as strong. But the Bible teaches that love is as strong as death (Song of Solomon 8:6). True love comes from God and this love was manifested toward us when He sent His only begotten Son into the world, that we might live through Him (1st John 4:7-9). We love because He loved us first (1st John 4:19). And His love is perfected in us when we love one another (1st John 4:12). In fact, when we obey His commandment to love one another, we show our love for Him (1st John 5:2-3). God never makes us obey but it is a choice.

I can remember years ago reading 1st Corinthians 13:4-7 and thinking how a person can possibly keep all these things. But then I realize these various aspects of love included in these verses characterize God the

Father, Son and Holy Spirit. In these verses, love as an activity and a behavior is described, not just an inner feeling or motivation. And every Believer must seek to grow in this kind of love. The Believer must regard himself as alive to Christ in righteousness and put on the new qualities that are prompted by Christian love (Colossians 3:12-17).

Apostle Paul wrote to the Saints and faithful ones in Christ in the book of Colossians about how he heard of their faith in Christ Jesus and of the love they had for all saints. He wrote, "Since we heard of your faith in Christ Jesus, and of the love which ye have to all the saints, for the hope, which is laid up for you in heaven, whereof ye heard before in the word of the truth of the gospel (Colossians 1:4-5). Notice how faith and love spring from the hope that is stored up for us in heaven. This hope is an anchor of our soul, both sure and steadfast (Hebrews 6:19). Do you see how faith, hope and love work together, but love is the greatest of all? Because without love faith and hope doesn't have a chance. True love is in the Spirit (Colossians 1:8). It is a love that prompts sincere prayers for one another. Paul gives us a great prayer to pray for each other in this letter to the Colossians. "For this cause we also, since the day we heard it, do not cease to pray for you, and to desire that ye might be filled with the knowledge of his will in all wisdom and spiritual understanding; That ye might walk worthy of the Lord unto all pleasing, being fruitful in every good work, and increasing in the knowledge of God; Strengthened with all might, according to his glorious power, unto all patience and longsuffering with joyfulness; Giving thanks unto the Father, which hath made us meet (fit) to be partakers of the inheritance of the saints in light: Who hath delivered us from the power of darkness, and hath translated us unto the kingdom of his dear Son: In whom we have redemption (been set free) through his blood, even the forgiveness (remission) of sins (Colossians 1:9-14)". Ephesians also records the faith in the Lord Jesus and love unto all the saints that Apostle Paul heard of, which prompted this prayer for them. "That the God of our Lord Jesus Christ, the Father of glory, may give unto you the Spirit of wisdom and revelation in the knowledge of him: the eyes of your understanding being enlightened; that ye may know what is the hope of his calling, and what the riches of the glory of his inheritance in the saints, and what is the exceeding greatness of his power to us-ward who believe, according to the working of his mighty power, Which he wrought in Christ, when he raised him from the dead, and set him at his own right hand in the heavenly places, Far above all principality, and power, and might, and dominion, and every name that is named, not only in this world, but also in that which is to come: And hath put all things under his feet, and gave him to be the head over all things to the church, Which is his body, the fulness of him that filleth all in all. (1:17-23). When true love is involved, our prayers will be genuine.

Yes, love is the greatest of all these. But how do we love according to the standard in which the Bible teaches? The answer to this question can found in Romans 5:5 – And hope does not put us to shame, because God's love has been poured out into our hearts through the Holy Spirit, who has been given to us (NIV). Notice that we have been given the Holy Spirit and He pours God's love into our hearts. The Holy Spirit within our hearts pours out the love of God into our hearts. There are times when I am in prayer, and I get the overwhelming presence of God's love in my heart. This is an ongoing process of the Holy Spirit pouring out this divine love into our hearts again and again. We experience the perfect love of God. We feel it and we accept it, and we know it. Love is core to God's character and central to the Christian life.

God so loved the world that He gave His only Song (John 3:16). Jesus came from heaven as the Son of God's love to show what love is, and He lived a life of love while here on earth in fellowship with His disciples, in compassion over the poor and miserable, even to His enemies and He died the death of love. And He commanded the disciples to love one another. Jesus also knew that the only way this would be possible was through the promise of the Holy Spirit. So, we are called to walk in love. The more of us that Holy Spirit possess, the more the heart will be filled with real, divine, universal love. Thus, there must be a denying of self once for all, daily for Holy Spirit to take possession of us. Christ comes to live in our hearts forever and the self-life is cast out. Never believe that it is impossible to do what God has commanded us to do because He gives us what we need to accomplish it. But we have to surrender and obey Holy Spirit in His leading. Jesus taught us that the greatest two commandments include love (Matthew 22:37-40). Love always requires an "other" as an object; love cannot remain within itself. The law of Christ is to love God and love others. The love that is poured out into our hearts by the Holy Spirit never fails (1st Corinthians 13:8). Anything that is contrary to love is not of the Holy Spirit. "Whoever does not love does not know God, because God is love." 1st John 4:8

The love of God is poured out in our hearts through the Holy Spirit. We should never try to love God or others with our natural love. We were Created with the capacity to love as God loves and through the regeneration, this love is our reality. It is the Holy Spirit who reveals the love of God in us, confirms His love, and assures us and with the love of God (2nd Timothy 1:7). Remember we love because He first loved us. (1st John 4:19).

"My purpose is that they may be encouraged in heart and united in love, so that they may have the full riches of complete understanding, in order that they may know the mystery of God, namely, Christ, in whom are hidden all the treasures of wisdom and knowledge." Colossians 2:2-3 NIV

Twenty

∽

The Symbols of The Holy Spirit

In the Bible, the Holy Spirit is represented by various symbols. These are just a few of the symbols. Each of these symbols depicted different attributes of His nature or His work. In the Old Testament, we know that the Holy Spirit hovered over the waters (Genesis1:2). He is referred to as the **wind** or breath of God. When the LORD God formed the man from the dust of the ground, He breathed into his nostrils the breath of life and the man became a living being (Genesis 2:7). The wind blows wherever it pleases. Although you hear the sound, you cannot detect where it comes from or where it is going (John 3:80). The Greek and Hebrew words for "spirit" are synonymous with "breath" or "wind". On The day of Pentecost, the outpouring of the Holy Spirit was accompanied by the sound of a mighty, rushing wind (Acts 2:2).

The **dove** is also a symbol of Holy Spirit. This symbol is probably the most familiar of the symbols. The dove is symbolic of the baptism of Jesus. As soon as He came up out of the water, the heaven opened, and the Spirit of God came upon Him like a dove and remained on Him (Matthew 3:16-17; Mark 1:10; Luke 3:22; John 1:32). The dove represents the gentleness, innocence, purity and patience of the Holy Spirit (Matthew 10:16; Psalm 68:13).

Holy Spirit is as a **seal** to express God's possession of the Believer.

Ephesians 1:13-14 states, "And you also were included in Christ when you heard the message of truth, the gospel of your salvation. When you believed, you were marked in him with a seal, the promised Holy Spirit, who is a deposit guaranteeing our inheritance until the redemption of those who are God's possession – to the praise of his glory." The seal of Holy Spirit is the Believer's security in Christ. It is proof that they belong to God forever (John 6:37; Ephesians 4:30; 2nd Corinthians 1:22).

Fire is another symbol of Holy Spirit's power and presence with emphasis on purification. Jesus baptizes with the Holy Spirit and fire (Matthew 3:11). On the day of Pentecost tongues of fire rested on the disciples and they were filled with the Holy Spirit (Acts 2:3-4).

Jesus stood up on the last day of the great feast and cried out, "If any man thirst, let him come unto me and drink. He that believes on me, as the scripture has said, out of his belly shall flow rivers of living water (John 7:37-38). He was talking about the Holy Spirit with the symbol of **water** (John 7:39). Water represents the life-giving power of God.

The Holy Spirit is like **oil**. Anointing oil is in direct correlation with the work of Holy Spirit. It is a sign of His approval, anointing and power. When Israel's kings and priests were anointed with oil it was a picture of God's choice and blessing. In the New Testament the anointing oil is a picture of the blessing of the Holy Spirit on believers. (1st Samuel 16:13; Isaiah 61:1; Luke 4:18; Acts 10:38).

Water represents the life-giving power of God. Jesus cried out, "If any man thirst, let him come unto me and drink (John 7:37). Holy Spirit is the rivers of living water that will flow from the belly of those who believe (John 7:38). Those that believe on Jesus will receive this water (John 7:39).

Clothing is also a symbol of the Holy Spirit. Jesus told His disciples to tarry in Jerusalem until they were clothed with the power of the Holy Spirit (Luke 24:49). I also believe He is also the garments of salvation and the robe of righteousness (Isaiah 61:10)

Twenty-One

꩜

The Outpouring of the Holy Spirit and the Global Release of God's Glory

To Advance the Kingdom of God

"...the One who fills the eternal realm with glory... **Isaiah 57:15**

It is God who fills the expanse of eternity with His glory. If He can do that, what can He do in our life. Our Creator of all that is seen, and unseen has held time and space safely in order without missing a beat or needing help. So why do we pick and choose what we think God can or can't; will or won't do? Why do we limit Him based on what we decide is a miracle on what we can wrap our mind around or accept? God wants to flood our lives with the same glory that fills the eternal realm. The glory that changes everything about the way we live our life and experience Him on a deeper spiritual level.

Some time ago, maybe around 2019, God had started talking to me about a global release of His glory and the outpouring of the Holy Spirit. I was given any details. I wasn't given a date or time. But since the emerging of this unclean spirit, this plague, Covid-19 (and all variants of the one virus), I can sense the closeness of this word. Not only that but I have heard a number of prophets in 2022 prophesying about the glory of God on a global level. God is giving confirmation after confirmation. I am in great expectation of the global release of the glory of God and the outpouring of the Holy Spirit. One of the main scriptures that I keep hearing is Isaiah 60:2: For behold, the darkness will cover the earth. Much darkness will cover the people. But the Lord will rise upon you, and His glory will be seen upon you (NKJV). The Amplified says "His glory and brilliance"; the English Translation (NET) says "His splendor"; the New Life Version (NLV) says "His shining-greatness"; the Orthodox Jewish Bible (OJB) says "His kavod". I do believe that for our era, we have seen the darkest time ever with this pandemic that effected and affect the globe. We have experienced darkness covering the earth like never before in our time and gross darkness the people. Therefore, it has set the stage for the glory of God to be released like never before. I believe that darkness will never overtake light, and light shines the brightest in the darkest of times.

I have read a number of definitions for the glory of God. I believe in trying to define the glory of God it will always be incomplete as our God can never be fully described by His human creation. Just as Moses could not see all of God's glory, so we won't be able to define His glory completely. Nevertheless, the glory of God is central to the gospel and everything He does. I believe the glory of God is the invisible qualities, character, or attributes of God displayed in a visible (or knowable) way. God's glory is His invisible character made visible. Isaiah 6:3 tells us, "Holy, Holy, Holy is the LORD of hosts; the whole earth is full of His glory!" In other words, God's glory is His character going public for the world to witness and know that He is God and God alone. There is none like Him.

According to the bible, the Glory of Gid is displayed supremely in the Jesus Christ. Hebrews 1:3 states, "He is the radiance of the glory of God and the exact imprint of His nature, and He upholds the universe by the word of His power. After making purification for sins, He sat down at the right hand of the Majesty on high." Then 2nd Corinthians 4:6 states, "For God, who said, "Let light shine out of darkness," has shone in our hearts to give the light of the knowledge of the glory of God in the face of Jesus Christ." In talking about the glory of God we must talk about the gospel of Jesus Christ. Why? Because more than anything else, God reveals Himself through what He does, through the finished work of the Cross and the Resurrection. The gospel is the apex of God's love and Christ is the apex image of the invisible God. In other words, what we know about God can be seen most clearly in Christ. In John 10:30, Jesus said, "I and My Father are one." Jesus Christ is God Himself (John 1:1). He is the Word who became flesh (John 1:14). He is He who became and made the invisible God visible (Colossians 1:15). Jesus Christ came to show us the exact imprint of God's nature (Hebrews 1:3). He came to show us the Father in Himself (John 14:7-14). Christ came that the love of God might be manifested (1st John 4:9). I submit to you that Jesus Christ, the Son of the Living God, is the glory of God. Jesus glorifies God the most because He reveals God the most.

What if the release the global release of God's Glory is the preaching of the Gospel of Jesus Christ? Habakkuk 2:14 tells us "For the earth shall be filled with the knowledge of the glory of the LORD, as the waters cover the sea." I am reminded of what is written in Matthew 24:14 – "And this gospel of the Kingdom shall be preached in all the world for a witness unto all nations; and then shall the end come." Is God preparing the stage for the coming of the end of the Church age by this global release? I believe He is building His Church, the Bride of Christ, from people all over the globe through faith in Christ Jesus in His time. Revelation 5:9 states, "...with Your blood You purchased for God persons from every tribe and language and people and nation." The purpose of the Church has not changed. God's plan through the Church is to "Go ye therefore, and teach all nations, baptizing them in the name of the Father, and of the Son, and of the Holy Ghost (Matthew 28:19). Now, I am don't believe this baptism isn't necessarily talking about water baptism but teaching and conversion as it follows up with verse 20 "Teaching them to observe all things whatsoever I have commanded you: and lo, I am with you always, even unto the end of the world." In other words, the great commission to the Church is to preach/teach the Gospel and convert people and make them disciples (Deny themselves, take up their cross and follow Jesus Christ). And the early Church did just that and God confirmed His word with signs and wonders. Mark 16:20 teaches: And they went forth, and preached everywhere, the Lord working with them, and confirming the word with signs and following. God has divinely enabled the Church to minister to people whether they be inside the church or out in the world, by the power of the Holy Spirit. Throughout Scripture, we read about the Holy Spirit anointing people to accomplish God's will and purposes in the earth.

Thus, this is where the outpouring of the Spirit comes in with the Global Release of His Glory. It will take the Outpouring of the Holy Spirit for there to be a Global Release of God's Glory. Remember Jesus promised His disciples that they would receive the Holy Spirit. Acts 1:8 states, "But ye shall receive power, after that the Holy Ghost is come upon you: and ye shall be witnesses unto me both in Jerusalem, and in all Judea, and in Samaria, and unto the uttermost part of the earth." The Holy Spirit wasn't just for the early Church but for the Church now. Peter preached this in Acts 2:39: For the promise is unto you, and to your children, and to all that are afar off, even as many as the Lord our God shall call. By the anointing of the Holy Spirit, the Church is called to advance the Kingdom of God – to empty hell and populate the God's Kingdom. Why? Because "The Lord is not slow to fulfil His promise as some count slowness, but is patient toward you, not wishing that any should perish, but that all should reach repentance." (2nd Peter 3:9).

Therefore, by the Holy Spirit, God has blessed the Church with gifts and callings to effectively minister to people's spiritual needs as well as to their physical needs. Now there are diversities of gifts, but the same the Spirit. And there are differences of administrations, but the same Lord. And there are diversities of operations, but it is the same God which worketh all in all. But the manifestation of the Spirit is given to every man to profit withal. For to one is given by the Spirit the word of wisdom; to another the work of knowledge by the same Spirit; To another faith by the same Spirit; to another the gifts of healing by the same Spirit; To another the working of miracles; to another prophecy; to another discerning of spirits, to another divers kinds of tongues; to another the interpretation of tongues: But all these worketh that one and the self-same Spirit, dividing to every man severally as He will (1st Corinthians 12:4-11). Again, God's purpose for the Church has not changed. God still has set some in the Church, first apostles; secondly prophets; thirdly teachers; after that, miracles; then gifts of healing; helps; governments; diversities of tongues. (1st Corinthians 12:28). Why? The answer is in Ephesians 4:11-12: So, Christ Himself gave the apostles, the prophets, the evangelists, the pastors and teachers, to equip His people for works of service, so that the body of Christ may be built up until we all reach unity in the faith and in the knowledge of the Son of God and become mature, attaining to the whole measure of the fullness of Christ. It is all about the knowledge of Jesus Christ. The Apostle Peter admonishes us: But grow in grace, and in the knowledge of our Lord and Savior Jesus Christ (2 Peter 3:18). When the Church desires the pure milk of the Word, she will indeed grow up in her salvation because she has tasted that the Lord is good (1st Peter 2:2-3). A sure sign of spiritual health is a deep desire to feed on the living and enduring Word of God.

I don't have all the details of the Global release of God's Glory or the outpouring of the Holy Spirit, but I do know that Christ is soon to return and there are certain preparations that has to take place before that happens. Therefore, I do pray the Lord of the harvest to send out laborers into His harvest (Matthew 9:38). It is God's desire for personal intimacy and when His glory shows up, it makes God real and personal. He is no longer the God who is a million miles away, but He is the God who comes down wanting to dwell among us and within us. There is no greater place then to be in God's presence enjoying His love and the joy of Holy Spirit. God wants to fill the earth with His glory. And we must cooperate with the Holy Spirit in fulfilling this desire to fill the earth with the Glory of God.

God still has plans to reveal His glory to His people, both as a Body and individually. Throughout the Old Testament, God was faithful to come down into the midst of His people in a corporate setting visiting them in power and glory. He is still God, and He still wants to bless His children with His presence and power. It is time for the glory of God to fill the house of God again. We need His glory in our churches and in our individual lives. **"Lord, show us Your Glory."**

Twenty-Two

~

Conclusion

"And if the Spirit of Him who raised Jesus from the dead is living in you, He who raised Christ from the dead will also give life to your mortal bodies because of His Spirit who lives in you." Romans 8:11

In writing as an inspirational author, I am aware that I can only be effective and fruitful as soul winners to the lost and encouragers to the saints of God as I am filled with the Holy Spirit and totally and exclusively rely on the power of God's Word. My greatest testimony of the gospel of salvation is that I have been transformed by the gospel of Jesus Christ. Thus, my witness is not something I do, but it is what I am.

The Gospel is my measuring rod of God's grace (Titus 2:11,15). Therefore, I must grow in understanding the doctrine of the Gospel. I understand what Apostle Paul meant in 1st Corinthians 2:2 when he said that he wanted to know Christ and Him crucified and the power of His resurrection. The Gospel is the power of God unto salvation and unto sanctification.

I truly believe that the overall approach to present the gospel of Jesus Christ that produces true converts, regenerated people, is to let people know that Jesus Christ willingly died for our sins (Romans 5:8). He was buried. He was raised by God from the dead. It has to be emphasized that the gospel of Jesus Christ is the only means of salvation. Through the demonstration of His grace and justice, God gave His Only Son to be our substitute. Literally. Jesus bore the judgment of God on our behalf. God judged Him instead of judging us.

The gospel has to be presented as God's Holy character which demands justice for our sin of unbelief. I understand that unbelief is not saying there is no God, but it is purposefully and willfully rejecting God's plan of salvation through His Son. I once read that unbelief is a state of mind that states, they don't need nor want God. In other words, I don't need salvation. Those who are truly born-again and who will be born again has the revelation that they see themselves as an offense towards God that has separated them from God. And that Jesus Christ is the Only solution or defense against it. Then the Holy Spirit will bring conviction of the sinful condition and rescued from the direr consequences of eternal torment being separated from God.

With all this in mind, I carefully and prayerfully seek to share this good news so that it can be perceived as foundational in what is offered by God and what is at stake. I believe the message of the good news of Jesus Christ has to be given as an ultimatum not as an alternative (John 3:17) because there is no other name under the heavens whereas men can be saved except the name of Jesus (Acts 4:12).

The Holy Spirit indwells Believers. Scripture teaches that all believers are indwelt by the Holy Spirit (1st Corinthians 6:19). This ministry of indwelling the Believer is to control the newly created nature given at conversion (2nd Corinthians 5:17; Ephesians 3:16).

The Holy Spirit fills Believers. We are admonished to "be filled with the Spirit" (Ephesians 5:18). Remember the word "fill" means to be controlled. The in filling does not mean that the Believer gets more of the Holy Spirit, but rather, He gets more or all of the Believer.

The Holy Spirit sanctifies the Believer (Romans 15:16; 2nd Thessalonians 2:13).

The Holy Spirit produces fruit in the life of the Believer (Galatians 5:22-23).

The Holy Spirit imparts gifts to Believers (Romans 12:6-8; 1ˢᵗ Corinthians 12:1-11; Ephesians 4:7-12). The purpose of these gifts is twofold, namely, to glorify God (Revelation 4:11) and edify the body of Christ (Ephesians 4:12-13).

The Holy Spirit teaches Believers. He will instruct us in all spiritual matters as we read the word of God (John 14:26).

God's purpose for us now is to live righteously and be ready for the coming of the Lord.

Matthew 24, 25; 1ˢᵗ Corinthians 15; 1ˢᵗ Thessalonians 4:13-5:11; 2ⁿᵈ Thessalonians 2; Hebrews 10:23-25; 2ⁿᵈ Peter 3

The Purpose: Matthew 28:18-20

The Power: Acts 1:8

The Prayer: Matthew 9:38

- God's plan of salvation is clear and concise
- Christ came to meet the need of humanity. – Salvation is for sinners only (Luke 5:32)
- Christ came to be the sinner's substitute – John 10:11
- Christ came to do what no one else could do (John 14:6) prepare me a body
- Christ came to provide assurance to those who put their trust in Him (Luke 7:48-50

This is the story of salvation in four Words

1. Sin
2. Calvary
3. Faith
4. Life

The proof of your salvation is not by sensation It is by faith in scripture

- Salvation is needed. Romans 3:23

- Salvation is provided. John 3:6 and 1st Peter 2:24
- Salvation is offered. Ephesians 2:8
- Salvation is accepted. 1st John 5:12

When a person passes from this life (time) to the next life (eternity) he cannot return for a second chance.

In the Person and finished work of the Lord Jesus Christ we have the message of hope, salvation and redemption.

There is a time, we know not when,
A place, we know not where,
Which marks the destiny of men
To glory or despair.
There is a line, by us unseen,
Which crosses every path.
Which marks the boundary between
God's mercy and His wrath
To pass that limit is to die,
To die as if by stealth,
It does not dim the beaming eye,
Nor pale the glow of health.
The conscience may be still at ease,
The spirit light and gay,
And that which pleases still may please,
And care be thrust away.
But on that forehead God hath set
Indelibly a mark,
Unseen by man, for man as yet,
Is blind and in the dark.
He feels perchance that all is well
And every fear is calmed;
He lives, He dies, he walks in hell,
Not only doomed, but damned!
O, where is that mysterious line

That may by men be crossed,
Beyond which God himself hath sworn,
That he who goes is lost?
An answer from the skies repeats,
Ye, who from God depart.
Today, O hear His voice,
Today repent and harden not your heart.
By **Joseph Addison Alexander**

Twenty-Three

～

Afterward

Each representative of Christ shares the message of Christ. But more, the true messenger "puts off", i.e., subordinates self-will by prioritizing the will of God. Dr. Bryant is passionate about God's charge to tell the world about God, one person at a time, about the love, forgiveness, and hope that Jesus Christ offers to everyone who surrenders to Him. "The Holy Spirit: The Promise. The Presence. The Power," Dr. Bryant's fifth message, acquaints us with God, the Holy Spirit. It is a great read. The personal anecdotes provide us points of inflection for self-reflection.

Don't just read "The Holy Spirit: The Promise. The Presence. The Power," *hagah* [meditate] on Scripture as it acquits you with the Holy Spirit. Having read the draft, I found myself reflecting on whether I readily engage the Holy Spirit as He comforts and guides me in my daily encounters and livings, whether my relating to others reveals that I am a believer, God's child, and surrendered to His guidance. Does your day start with prayer? Are you putting on the full armor of God before you get out of bed each morning? Does your day continue in prayer?

As Dr. Bryant admits, being Jesus' representative is not easy. Business representatives may need to showcase their products to a buyer that believes he is already satisfied or well served by his current supplier. That is not an easy sale to make. As followers of Christ, we are charged to share

Christ's message of repentance and forgiveness to all people. We are called to love and pray for our enemies, definitely not a simple task. Even if we do not perceive the person we are talking with as an enemy on the surface, we must always remember that those who are not Christians are by their sinful nature enemies of Christ. They need our love and prayers. They are lost, so very lost, even when they think their current life has served them well. This is a battle fought on the spiritual level. God, the Holy Spirit, prepares us for and guides those surrendered through conflict, but does not instigate it.

Using pragmatic language and narrative, Dr. Bryant reiterates that when we allow God to change our hearts, we see our mission more clearly. We see the hearts and the hurts of our neighbors, our co-workers, and the people we meet in the store or at the park. It is only because of God's grace that we have been saved, and only through His grace that anyone is saved. It is God's work to save the lost. Our job is to be obedient and be His representatives in this lost and dying world.

Enjoy reading read "The Holy Spirit: The Promise. The Presence. The Power."

Gerald Seals, D. Div., Ph.D.
Pastor, Living Word Church and Fellowship

Twenty-Four

cɲɔ

From Dr. Mary J. Bryant

I never want to grieve or quench the Holy Spirit. I love the Holy Spirit. I need Him!!!

I am totally humbled to be given the grace to once again embark on another publishing journey with the LORD. This book, **Holy Spirit: The Promise. The Presence. The Power.**, is my 5th inspirational book. I count it a privilege and honor to write such a purposeful and powerful book. I can attest to the promise, the presence, and the power would not be here today if it wasn't for Holy Spirit. He came to me as my Counsellor and Comforter when I didn't know to call Him. He came to me as my Teacher and Revelation-Light of the Word of God. I know Him to be my Advocate in this new life. I am so beyond grateful to Him for pursing me, convicting me, correcting me, discipling me and chastening me when needed and necessary. I am grateful that He leads and guides in this new life in Christ with such love and compassion I am grateful that He cultivates the fruit of the Spirit in me in all goodness, righteousness, and truth (Ephesians 5:9) to approve what is acceptable unto the LORD.

This book by no means replaces the Bible but it is my way of advancing the Kingdom of God. It is my sincere prayer that according to Acts 26:18 it will help open eyes, and turn people from darkness to light, and from the power of Satan unto the power of God, that they may receive forgiveness of sins, and inheritance among those which are sanctified by faith that in Christ Jesus [by Holy Spirit].

I thank God for sending Holy Spirit back to earth to be a witness unto Christ for those who believe and receive Christ by faith. When we are baptized in the Spirit, we receive power to witness for Christ, the same Spirit that descended on Jesus and raised Him from the dead.

May our speech, attitude and action in all things reveal that we are the children of God, filled with His Spirit to live this victorious life in the LORD as overcomers, and empowered to for service. May we always give thanks for all things unto God and the Father in the name of our LORD Jesus Christ." (Ephesians 5:20)

At God's Right Hand,
Mary J. Bryant

Let Spirit of Christ be in your heart,
Eternity in your spirit,
The world under your feet,
The will of God in your actions,
And let the love of God shine forth from you.

Do you want to know how you can receive, experience, and enjoy the all-inclusive Christ as the all-inclusive life-giving Spirit? It is by receiving the Spirit through faith daily and being supplied by the Spirit in your daily living.

- By God's revealing of Christ in us (Galatians 1:16a, Ephesians 1:17; 3:8-19).
- By our receiving of Christ out of the hearing of faith (Galatians 3:2).
- By being born according to the Spirit and by being given the Spirit of God's Son into our hearts (Galatians 4:29b; 6).

- By putting on Christ through the baptism that puts us into Christ (Galatians 3:27).
- By being identified with Him in His death so that it may be no longer we who live but He who lives in us (Galatians 2:20).
- By living and walking by the Spirit (Galatians 5:16, 25).
- By having Christ formed in us through travail (Galatians 4:19).
- By sowing unto the Spirit with the desire and aim of the Spirit in view, to accomplish what the Spirit desires (Galatians 6:7-8).
- By boasting in the cross of Christ and living a new creation (Galatians 6:14-15).
- By enjoying the grace of the Lord Jesus Christ with our spirit (Galatians 6:17-18).

Hallelujah! Simply, you can receive the Spirit through faith, not through works of the law; you can exercise your spirit to enjoy the bountiful supply of the Spirit through faith, not through anything that you can do for God out of yourselves. Be blessed.

"He therefore who bountifully supplies to you the Spirit and does works of power among you, does He do it out of the works of laws or out of the hearing of faith?" Galatians 3:5

Twenty-Five

About the author

Dr. Mary J. Bryant is an inspirational writer. She has had several articles published: Hope for Today and Tomorrow and The Battle Belongs to the Lord. She also writes for her blog: www.doveministry378.blog-spot.com.

Holy Spirit: The Promise. The Presence. The Power is Mary's fifth inspirational book. Her first book is titled Prayers, Poems, and Precious Moments. It is not surprising that after writing such a transparent and intimate book of her relationship with Jesus in her first book, Prayers, Poems and Precious Moments, that she has continued to write these inspirational books. She has a love for God's Word and the earnest desire for the saints of God to rise to their greatest potential through the knowledge of our Lord Jesus Christ and applying it to our everyday lives. She believes that God wants the Body of Christ to walk in victory in every area of life by the power of the Holy Spirit.

taken by Michael Bryant

Mary's goal is to cease to exist in her opinions, her agendas, her goals, her desires, and her selfish choices. It is her sincere and urgent desire to surrender her will to the Lord's will. In addition, deny herself, take up her cross daily by faith and follow Christ Jesus. Mary absolutely relies on the power of the Holy Spirit so that no one will trust in her wisdom but the power of God. First Corinthians 2:1-5 "...I relied only on the power of the Holy Spirit so they will not trust in human wisdom but the power of God.

Her prayer is that she may be holy, humble, zealous and patient walking in love. She prays that she will be an example and a blessing unto others and that God gets the glory. She reminds us "those who does not long to know more of Christ knows nothing of Him, **Yet**. A favorite Scripture of hers is "Now may the God of peace, who through the blood of the eternal covenant brought back from the dead our Lord Jesus, that great Shepherd of the sheep, equip you with everything good for doing His will, and may He work in us what is pleasing to Him, through Jesus Christ, to whom be glory for ever and ever. Amen." Hebrews 13:20-21

She also prays that she lives a life worthy of the Lord and to please Him in every way while bearing fruit in every good work, growing in the knowledge of God.

Her Mission is **to Glorify God, Edify the Body of Christ and Show the lost to the Cross and Christians to maturity.**

Twenty-Six

~

Other Books

Other Inspirational Books	Children's Books
Prayers, Poems, and Precious Moments	Marquis Finds a Friend
I Recommend Jesus	Marquis Goes to the Circus
New Life in Christ by Faith	Marquis Gets a Bicycle for Christmas
You are God Alone	

You may contact the author at: doveministry378@yahoo.com
Social Media

- Faith in Action Show on YouTube
- Instagram/ faith378action
- Facebook/ @nowfaith378
- Twitter/ @maryj378
- Blog/ doveministry378.blogspot.com

www.ingramcontent.com/pod-product-compliance
Lightning Source LLC
Chambersburg PA
CBHW071759120626
46550CB00002B/853